HSC

DAVID C⟨

NOTES

including
- *Life of the Author*
- *Brief Synopsis of the Novel*
- *List of Characters*
- *Summaries and Commentaries*
- *Selected Bibliography*

by
J. M. Lybyer
Washington University

Hungry Minds™

Best-Selling Books • Digital Downloads • e-Books • Answer Networks • e-Newsletters • Branded Web Sites • e-Learning

New York, NY • Cleveland, OH • Indianapolis, IN

CliffsNotes™ David Copperfield

Published by:
Hungry Minds, Inc.
909 Third Avenue
New York, NY 10022

www.hungryminds.com
www.cliffsnotes.com (CliffsNotes Web site)

ISBN: 0-8220-0364-3

Printed in the United States of America

10 9 8 7 6 5 4

1V/QV/RQ/QS/IN

Distributed in the United States by Hungry Minds, Inc.

Distributed by CDG Books Canada Inc. for Canada; by Transworld Publishers Limited in the United Kingdom; by IDG Norge Books for Norway; by IDG Sweden Books for Sweden; by IDG Books Australia Publishing Corporation Pty. Ltd. for Australia and New Zealand; by TransQuest Publishers Pte Ltd. for Singapore, Malaysia, Thailand, Indonesia, and Hong Kong; by Gotop Information Inc. for Taiwan; by ICG Muse, Inc. for Japan; by Norma Comunicaciones S.A. for Columbia; by Intersoft for South Africa; by Eyrolles for France; by International Thomson Publishing for Germany, Austria and Switzerland; by Distribuidora Cuspide for Argentina; by LR International for Brazil; by Galileo Libros for Chile; by Ediciones ZETA S.C.R. Ltda. for Peru; by WS Computer Publishing Corporation, Inc., for the Philippines; by Contemporanea de Ediciones for Venezuela; by Express Computer Distributors for the Caribbean and West Indies; by Micronesia Media Distributor, Inc. for Micronesia; by Grupo Editorial Norma S.A. for Guatemala; by Chips Computadoras S.A. de C.V. for Mexico; by Editorial Norma de Panama S.A. for Panama; by American Bookshops for Finland. Authorized Sales Agent: Anthony Rudkin Associates for the Middle East and North Africa.

For general information on Hungry Minds' products and services please contact our Customer Care department; within the U.S. at 800-762-2974, outside the U.S. at 317-572-3993 or fax 317-572-4002.

For sales inquiries and resellers information, including discounts, premium and bulk quantity sales and foreign language translations please contact our Customer Care department at 800-434-3422, fax 317-572-4002 or write to Hungry Minds, Inc., Attn: Customer Care department, 10475 Crosspoint Boulevard, Indianapolis, IN 46256.

For information on licensing foreign or domestic rights, please contact our Sub-Rights Customer Care department at 212-884-5000.

For information on using Hungry Minds' products and services in the classroom or for ordering examination copies, please contact our Educational Sales department at 800-434-2086 or fax 317-572-4005.

Please contact our Public Relations department at 212-884-5163 for press review copies or 212-884-5000 for author interviews and other publicity information or fax 212-884-5400.

For authorization to photocopy items for corporate, personal, or educational use, please contact Copyright Clearance Center, 222 Rosewood Drive, Danvers, MA 01923, or fax 978-750-4470.

Hungry Minds™ is a trademark of Hungry Minds, Inc.

CONTENTS

DAVID COPPERFIELD NOTES

LIFE OF THE AUTHOR

Charles Dickens (1812-70) was born in Portsmouth, on the south coast of England, but his family moved to Chatham while he was still very young. His most pleasant childhood years were spent in Chatham, and re-creations of these scenes appear in a disguised form in many of his novels. His father, John Dickens, was a minor clerk in the Navy Pay Office and, like Mr. Micawber in *David Copperfield*, was constantly in debt.

In 1822, John Dickens was transferred to London, but debts continued to pile up, and the family was forced to sell household items in order to pay some of the creditors. Young Charles made frequent trips to the pawnshop, but eventually his father was arrested and sent to debtors' prison, and at the age of twelve, he was sent to work in a blacking warehouse, where he pasted labels on bottles for six shillings a week. This experience was degrading for the young boy, and Dickens later wrote: "No words can express the secret agony of my soul. I felt my early hopes of growing up to be a learned and distinguished man, crushed in my breast." The situation is an exact parallel to David Copperfield's plight at the wine warehouse. Even after his father was released from prison and the family inherited some money, his mother wanted him to continue with his job.

Later, for two and a half years, Dickens attended school at Wellington House Academy, and then in 1827, at the age of fifteen, he began work as a clerk in a law office and taught himself shorthand so he could report court debates. At the same time, he was learning about life in London and frequently attended the theater, even taking acting lessons for a short time.

Meanwhile, Dickens had fallen in love with Maria Beadnell, a frivolous young girl whose father objected to his daughter's being courted by a young reporter from a lower middle-class background. Nothing came of this relationship, but it probably intensified

Dickens' efforts to make something of himself. In 1832, he began working as a parliamentary reporter for two London newspapers, and two years later, he joined a new paper, the *Morning Chronicle*, where he was asked to write a series of sketches about London life. This request resulted in *Sketches by Boz*, which appeared in installments that were later, in 1836, published in book form. Dickens' career as an author was begun. This led to an offer to write a monthly newspaper series about a group of humorous English clubmen. These pieces became *The Posthumous Papers of the Pickwick Club*, and after they appeared, Dickens' reputation as a writer was assured.

He now felt financially secure and quit his job as a parliamentary reporter to devote all his time to writing. He married Catherine Hogarth in April, 1836; however, the marriage was never a happy one and Dickens separated from his wife twenty years later.

His writing output increased, and a number of novels, including *Oliver Twist* and *Nicholas Nickleby*, were published—first in monthly installments and then as novels. By the 1840s, Dickens was the most popular writer in England. In 1849, he began one of his most important novels, *David Copperfield*. His friend John Forster proposed that he tell the story in the first person, and this suggestion proved to be a perfect method for Dickens to fictionalize the background of his early life. David Copperfield became the "favorite child" of its author and in it Dickens transcribed his own experiences, producing not only a fine novel, but a disguised autobiography as well.

But the novel is not pure biography; rather, it is Dickens' experiences made into fiction. In the novel, David escapes from the warehouse to a sympathetic aunt, and he marries Dora after the "timely" death of her father. This did not happen in real life, and it is almost as though Dickens were reconstructing parts of his childhood the way he wished it had been. In the novel, too, Dickens shows his contempt for his parents (in the guise of the Murdstones) for sending him to the blacking factory, and, at the same time, his devotion to them (the Micawber family) as lovable eccentrics. Dora Spenlow becomes both Maria Beadnell and, later, the simple-minded Catherine Hogarth, his real wife. The novel, thus, is both fantasy and fact.

Little needs to be said about the humor in the novel; it is simply to be enjoyed. The scene at the inn where the waiter eats David's dinner, the night of revelry when David becomes drunk and falls down the stairs, the preposterous Micawber boarding the ship with a telescope under his arm—all are near-slapstick pieces of good fun, and it is easy to understand the continuing popularity of the novel.

After *David Copperfield*, Dickens wrote novels that were bitter and caustic. *Bleak House* is a brooding satire on the law courts, while both *Hard Times* and *Little Dorrit* suffer from uncontrolled social outrage. The wildly humorous characters of Sam Weller, of *The Pickwick Papers*, and Mr. Micawber give way to dark, sinister figures, and although the later novels perhaps show more craftsmanship, most readers feel that the "magic" had worn off.

During the last years of his life, Dickens traveled in England and America, giving public readings from his works. The strain weakened his health, and he died in 1870 at the age of fifty-eight. At the time of his death, he was working on a novel, *The Mystery of Edwin Drood*, and though many writers have attempted to supply an ending, the book remains unfinished.

BRIEF SYNOPSIS OF THE NOVEL

The novel traces the life of David Copperfield from the time of his birth to his mature manhood, when he is married and familiar with the vicissitudes of life. His early years are enjoyable with his mother—who was widowed shortly before his birth—and with her servant, Peggotty. Life is happy for David until his mother decides to marry Mr. Murdstone; afterward, life becomes unbearable for David. He is soon sent to a miserable school where he becomes friendly with James Steerforth, a fellow student.

When David's mother dies, he is taken from school and put to work by Mr. Murdstone in a London warehouse. Although David enjoys the company of the impoverished Micawber family, with whom he boards, his other associates and the work are intolerable, so, without money or property, he runs away to his Aunt Betsey Trotwood in Dover. Despite a stern exterior, Aunt Betsey treats him well, adopting him and sending him to a good school. While at school, he boards with a Mr. Wickfield and his daughter Agnes. (Throughout the novel, David retains a fond, sisterly affection for Agnes.) After graduation, David works in the law office of Spenlow & Jorkins and soon falls in love with Mr. Spenlow's daughter, Dora.

About this time, Em'ly, the Peggottys' beloved niece, runs off to marry Steerforth, whom David had innocently introduced to her while she was engaged to Ham, a nephew of the Peggottys. The family is saddened by this development, but Mr. Peggotty sets out to find her and bring her back. David uses his spare time doing clerical and literary work to help Aunt Betsey, who now finds herself without financial resources. He marries Dora, only to find that he has a "child-wife" who knows nothing of housekeeping and cannot accept any responsibility.

Meanwhile, Uriah Heep, an "umble" clerk in Mr. Wickfield's employ, whom David dislikes, has deceitfully worked his way into a partnership, aided by Mr. Wickfield's weakness for wine. In addition, David also discovers that his old friend Mr. Micawber has gone to work for Heep. David has remained fond of the Micawbers, and it troubles him that his old friend is working for a scoundrel. Eventually, however, Micawber has a grand moment of glory when he exposes Heep as a fraud, helping to save Mr. Wickfield and restoring some of Aunt Betsey's finances.

David's wife, Dora, becomes ill and dies, and David is troubled until Em'ly, the Peggottys' niece, returns to her uncle. David has felt guilty for some time for having introduced Em'ly to Steerforth. After a reconciliation is accomplished, Em'ly, along with some of the Peggottys, and the Micawbers leave for Australia to begin new lives. Before they leave, David witnesses a dramatic shipwreck in which Steerforth is killed, as is Ham in attempting to rescue him. Still saddened by the loss of his wife and other events, David goes abroad for three years. It is only after he returns that he realizes that Agnes Wickfield has been his true love all along, and their happy marriage takes place at last.

LIST OF CHARACTERS

MAJOR CHARACTERS

David Copperfield

He is the central character in the novel and tells the story of his life from birth to adulthood. David is a sensitive youth who first suffers under the cruel Murdstones and then is sent away to work in a wine warehouse. David first marries Dora Spenlow, an empty-headed young girl; afterward, he realizes how incompatible they really are. When Dora dies, he marries Agnes Wickfield and by the novel's end, he has matured into a successful writer and adult.

Clara Copperfield

David's mother. She is an attractive, tender person, but impractical and emotional and easily taken in by Mr. Murdstone, who marries her because he is interested in her annuity.

Clara Peggotty

The Copperfields' housekeeper, who also acts as David's nurse. She is a woman of intense loyalty and is David's only companion after his mother's death. Peggotty marries Barkis, the cart-driver, and continues throughout the novel to be David's friend.

Edward Murdstone

David's stepfather. A dark, handsome man who cruelly beats David and slowly drives David's mother to an early death.

Jane Murdstone

Mr. Murdstone's sister. She runs the Copperfield household and incessantly harasses David.

Mr. Barkis

The driver of the horse-cart that travels between Yarmouth and David's home. He is a shy, quiet man who uses David as a messenger in his courtship of Peggotty.

Mr. Chillip

The doctor who delivers David. He is an exceedingly mild-mannered, frightened little man who is especially afraid of David's aunt, Betsey Trotwood.

Daniel Peggotty

Clara Peggotty's brother and a Yarmouth fisherman. He is a warm-hearted man whose house is a refuge for anyone who needs help.

Ham Peggotty

Mr. Peggotty's orphaned nephew. Ham, like his uncle, is a considerate, kindly person. He is in love with Em'ly and waits patiently for her after she runs away. He finally dies in an attempt to save Steerforth, Emily's seducer.

Little Em'ly

Mr. Peggotty's orphaned niece. She is David's childhood sweetheart, but becomes engaged to Ham and later runs away with Steerforth. She is a quiet, compassionate young girl who wants to become a "lady," a desire that leads to unhappiness.

Mrs. Gummidge

The widow of Mr. Peggotty's partner. She constantly complains about her hardships, but when Em'ly runs away, she changes into a helpful, inspiring confidante of Mr. Peggotty.

Charles Mell

A schoolmaster at the Salem House boarding school. A gentle friend and teacher of David.

Mr. Creakle

The sadistic headmaster of the Salem House School. He is a fiery-faced man who enjoys flogging the boys with a cane. He later becomes a prison magistrate.

Mr. Tungay

The assistant and cruel companion of Mr. Creakle. He has a wooden leg and repeats everything that Creakle says.

James Steerforth

A spoiled young man whom David admires. He has a surface polish and the good manners that deceive people who do not know him. His true selfishness is shown when he deserts Em'ly, leaving her with his servant, Littimer. He is killed in a storm off Yarmouth along with Ham, who tries to save him.

Tommy Traddles

David's friend. Of all the boys at the Salem House School, Traddles receives the most punishment. He is a good-natured, loyal friend to both David and Mr. Micawber. Traddles is persistent, and this quality helps him rise from his humble background to become a judge.

Wilkins Micawber

A constantly impoverished, but always optimistic, gentleman who boards David during his stay in London. He is a broad comic character with a passion for writing flowery letters and uttering grandiloquent speeches. He finally accompanies Mr. Peggotty to Australia, where he becomes a successful magistrate.

Emma Micawber

Mr. Micawber's long-suffering wife. She stands by her husband through all his hardships, even joining him in debtors' prison.

Betsey Trotwood

David's great-aunt. She is unhappy that David was born a boy instead of a girl, but later she acts as his guardian and provider during his early years of schooling. Her formal, often brisk, nature is deceiving; she is basically a sympathetic person.

Richard Babley (Mr. Dick)

A lovable simpleton cared for by Betsey Trotwood. He is engaged in writing a long manuscript that he uses to paper a huge kite. Mr. Dick is devoted to David's aunt and becomes a great friend of David's.

Uriah Heep

A repulsive, scheming young man who attempts to marry Agnes Wickfield and gain control of her father's law practice. He pretends to be humble and uses this as a means to gain vindictive revenge on people he believes have snubbed him. He is exposed by Mr. Micawber and ends up in prison.

Mr. Wickfield

A solicitor and the widowed father of Agnes Wickfield. He is a proud man, but his excessive drinking allows Uriah Heep to take advantage of him.

Agnes Wickfield

The daughter of Mr. Wickfield; David's second wife. She is a dutiful companion and housekeeper to her father and a sisterly friend to David while he stays at the Wickfield house. She proves to be a perfect wife and an inspiration to David in his writing.

Dr. Strong

The headmaster of the school which David attends in Canterbury. He is a scholarly, trusting gentleman who is married to a girl much younger than himself. Although his wife is accused of infidelity, he maintains his faith in her.

Annie Strong

Dr. Strong's youthful wife. She is a beautiful, affectionate girl whose family exploits her husband.

Jack Maldon

Annie Strong's cousin. He is a lazy, vain young man who tries to compromise Mrs. Strong, but is repulsed.

Mrs. Markleham

Annie Strong's mother. A forceful, selfish woman, she always takes Jack Maldon's part and unwittingly helps cause the misunderstanding between her daughter and Dr. Strong.

Mrs. Steerforth

James Steerforth's mother. A possessive woman who has spoiled her son by over-indulgence and a smothering affection; she lapses into a semi-invalid state when she hears of her son's death.

Rosa Dartle

Mrs. Steerforth's companion. She is a neurotic, quick-tempered young woman with a consuming love for Steerforth.

Littimer

Steerforth's personal manservant. He is a formal, haughty person who has an air of respectability, yet he aids Steerforth in his seduction of Em'ly. He is trapped by Miss Mowcher and is sent to Creakle's prison.

Miss Mowcher

A middle-aged dwarf who is a hairdresser for wealthy families. She is upset when she realizes that she was duped into helping Steerforth run off with Em'ly, and is instrumental in the capture of Littimer, who aided Steerforth.

Martha Endell

Em'ly's friend. She is a suffering woman who is forced to go to London to hide her shame. Martha redeems herself by saving Em'ly from a similar life and finds happiness in her own life after she arrives in Australia.

Mr. Spenlow

A proctor and partner in a law firm in Doctor's Commons. He is a pompous, aristocratic lawyer who objects to David's plans to marry his daughter.

Dora Spenlow

David's first wife. She is an impractical, empty-headed girl who cannot cook or manage a household. Although she is a poor selection as a wife, David is so taken by her childlike beauty that he overlooks her faults and marries her. Their marriage is a comedy of mismanagement until Dora dies, leaving David free to marry the domestically perfect Agnes.

MINOR CHARACTERS

Mr. Omer

The Yarmouth undertaker and dealer in funeral clothes.

Minnie Omer

Mr. Omer's daughter and Em'ly's working companion.

Joram

Minnie Omer's sweetheart and eventually her husband, and finally, Mr. Omer's business partner.

Mr. Quinion

A business associate of Mr. Murdstone.

Janet

Betsey Trotwood's housekeeper. She assists Miss Trotwood in chasing donkey riders off the lawn.

Mr. Jorkins

Mr. Spenlow's seldom-seen partner. He is reputed to be a strict businessman, but he is really a mild-mannered individual whose name is used to frighten new employees.

Julia Mills

Dora's girl friend. She is a romantic person who advises David in his courtship with Dora.

Mrs. Crupp

David's landlady. She is a lazy woman who drinks David's brandy and feuds with Aunt Betsey.

Sophy Crewler

Traddles' sweetheart. A patient girl from a large family, she marries Traddles and assists him in his work as a lawyer.

SUMMARIES AND COMMENTARIES

CHAPTERS 1-2

Summary

David was born in the "Rookery," in Blunderstone, Suffolk, England, on a Friday just as the clock began to strike midnight. This was thought to be an unlucky omen by some women of the neighborhood and by the nurse who attended his birth. A few hours before David's birth, however, Mrs. Copperfield is unexpectedly visited by Miss Betsey Trotwood, an aunt of David's father whom Mrs. Copperfield has never met. Miss Trotwood, "the principal magnate of our family," is a domineering woman who immediately takes charge of the household and insists that the expected child will be a girl; she declares that the new baby *girl* will be named Betsey Trotwood Copperfield. "There must be no mistakes in life with *this* Betsey Trotwood," she says. "I must make that *my* care."

Already agitated by the impending birth of this new baby, and by the death of David's father six months before, Mrs. Copperfield is further troubled by the abrupt appearance and manner of Miss Trotwood. She becomes ill with labor pains, and Ham, the nephew of the servant, Peggotty, is sent to get the doctor, Mr. Chillip. The mild-mannered Chillip is astonished, as is everyone else, by the brusqueness of Miss Trotwood. Later, when he tells her the baby is a *boy*, she silently but swiftly puts on her bonnet, walks out of the house, and vanishes "like a discontented fairy."

In Chapter 2, David recalls his home and its vast and mysterious passageways, the churchyard where his father is buried, Sundays in church, and his early life with his youthful, pretty mother and the kindly, capable Peggotty.

One night, after David learned to read, he is reading a story to Peggotty, and he asks, "if you marry a person, and the person dies, why then you may marry another person, mayn't you?" Almost immediately afterward, his mother enters the house with a bearded man whom David resents at once. After the stranger's departure, David hears an argument between his mother and Peggotty about the man. Peggotty insists that the man, Mr. Murdstone, is not an acceptable suitor.

About two months later, Peggotty invites David to spend a fortnight with her at her brother's place at Yarmouth. David is eager to go, but he asks what his mother will say. "She can't live by herself, you know," he insists. Young as he is, he does not realize that he is being sent away deliberately. His mother has a tearful farewell with him. As David and Peggotty drive off in a cart, David looks back. He sees Mr. Murdstone come up to his mother and apparently scold her for being so emotional.

Commentary

The first chapter is typical of the Victorian novelistic style, especially its long sentences and frequent digressions. The second paragraph is a long single sentence containing eighty-nine words (many sentences are longer). This chapter, and indeed the entire novel, frequently wanders from the main story line. The fourth paragraph of the book is a long digression on David's being born with a caul (a membrane that covers the head of a new-born child and was thought to bring good luck) and on his family's attempt to dispose of it profitably. After a lengthy detour, David pulls himself back to his narrative with an admonition to himself not to "meander." These stylistic features were the result of the publishing practices prevalant at Dickens' time. Books were first published serially in magazines and writers were paid by the word; hence, they included as many words as possible, even if the story became rambling and excessively wordy.

The first chapter also illustrates Dickens' handling of characterization. Dickens is often criticized for creating caricatures rather than characters in his works, of producing people who are one-dimensional and unreal. Both Miss Trotwood and the doctor are described extravagantly, but it must be remembered that this burlesque produces a humorous effect, and most readers of the time accepted the "overdone" quality, preferring entertainment to realism. David's mother and the servant girl, Peggotty, are described with greater restraint.

The character of Mr. Murdstone is strongly caught in Chapter 2. His name itself, compounded of "murder" and "stone," is typical of Dickens' device of creating an artificial name to reflect a person's character. As this chapter ends, the lines are drawn—David and Peggotty are hostile to Mr. Murdstone; Mrs. Copperfield, on the other hand, flattered and naive, is grateful for his attentions.

CHAPTERS 3-4

Summary

Ham, Peggotty's nephew who was present at David's birth, is waiting for them at a Yarmouth public-house and leads them to the hulk of an old ship drawn up on land; it has been renovated into a sort of "real home" and that is where the Peggotty family lives. Although everything has a strong odor of fish, the boat is clean, and David's room (in the stern of the barge) is the "most desirable bedroom ever seen."

David is introduced to Mr. Peggotty, a bachelor brother who is the head of the house. David is puzzled about the relationship of Ham and of Em'ly (a young girl who lives there and is a little younger than David); he learns from Peggotty that they are both orphan children of relatives who died at sea.

The next morning before breakfast, David and Em'ly play on the beach and Em'ly tells him about her fear of the sea because it has taken so many of her relatives. She runs out on a timber jutting from the side of the pier where the water is deepest and David becomes alarmed that she will fall in. He comments much later that he has never forgotten this episode, and he wonders if it might not have been better if she had drowned while she was young and innocent. They return from the beach with shells that they have collected, and they exchange an innocent kiss before going to eat. David feels certain that he is in love.

The holiday ends, and David and Peggotty return home by the same carrier's cart. David is sad at having to leave Yarmouth, but he looks forward to seeing his mother once more. He is not met by his mother, however; he is met by a strange servant, and for a minute David is afraid something has happened to his mother. Peggotty takes David to the kitchen and admits that she should have told him earlier what has happened—David's mother has remarried; David has a new "Pa." He is then led into the parlor to meet Mr. Murdstone.

In Chapter 4, Dickens focuses on David's unhappiness. David thinks of little Em'ly and cries himself to sleep. In the morning, Peggotty and David's mother come to his room, and his mother accuses Peggotty of prejudicing the boy against her and her new husband. Mr. Murdstone appears and cautions his wife about the need for "firmness" in handling David. He sends both women from the room, but not before scolding Peggotty for addressing her mistress by her *former* name. "She has taken *my* name," he says, "Will you remember that?" Mr. Murdstone says farther that unless David's manner improves he will be whipped with a strap.

After dinner, a coach arrives; Miss Murdstone, the sister of David's stepfather, has come to stay with the family. She is as hard and as austere a person as her brother, and she promptly informs everyone that *she* doesn't like *boys*. She observes that David *obviously* needs training with his manners, then immediately preempts the household keys and assumes all authority for running the household affairs. By degrees, she and her brother begin to intimidate David's mother until she becomes virtually an outsider in her own home.

One morning when David reports for his lessons, Mr. Murdstone is already there—with a cane, which he "poised and switched in the air." When the lesson goes badly, David is paraded upstairs, and his stepfather beats him, but not before David is able to literally bite the hand that feeds him (and in this case, restrains him). David is confined to his room for five days like a prisoner, and he is allowed out only for morning exercises and evening prayers. On the fifth day, Peggotty steals up to the room and speaks to David through the keyhole, informing him that tomorrow he is to be sent to a school near London.

The next morning David is sent away to school in the familiar horse-drawn cart. His grieving mother first implores him to "pray to be better," and then she blurts out, "I forgive you, my dear boy. God bless you!"

Commentary

The stay at Peggotty's home is one of the most idyllic experiences in David's life. The simple warmth of the poor family is in contrast to the coldness that David will encounter in his own home. Mr. Peggotty is a friendly man who sums himself up with his introductory phrase to David: "You'll find us rough, sir, but you'll find us ready." He is contrasted with Mrs. Gummidge, who lives there, and her often-repeated complaint: "I am a lone lorn creetur' and everythink goes contrairy with me." Dickens' characters invariably have one pet saying that, along with their names, indicates their personalities. Mrs. Gummidge later shows another side of her personality.

Note in Chapter 3 that Dickens foreshadows coming events when he says that it might have been "better for little Em'ly to have had the waters close above her head that morning. . . ." This effect is overly melodramatic perhaps, but it is a common technique of Victorian novelists to sustain reader interest over the course of a long narrative.

CHAPTERS 5-6

Summary

Before the cart goes half a mile it stops, and Peggotty appears from behind a hedgerow. Without saying a word, she hugs David and gives him some cakes to eat and a purse containing money, the coins wrapped in a note in his mother's handwriting, saying, "For Davy. With my love."

Mr. Barkis, the cart driver (who is as slow moving as the horse he drives), consoles David, and during the ride David offers him one of the cakes which Barkis eats "at one gulp exactly like an elephant." Mr. Barkis shyly inquires about Peggotty's cooking and asks if she has any "sweethearts." When David replies that she does not, the cart driver asks David to inform Peggotty that "Barkis is willin' "—a message David does not understand. (Later, David includes this unusual marriage proposal from Barkis in a letter to Peggotty.)

David sleeps in the cart until they reach Yarmouth, the first stage on his journey to London. Mr. Barkis drops David at an inn where eating arrangements have been made for him under the name of "Murdstone." He is served dinner, but the waiter tells him frightening stories about the food and then proceeds to eat most of David's meal himself.

The trip continues all night, but David is unable to sleep in the crowded coach. In the morning they reach London, "fuller of wonders and wickedness than all the cities of the earth," but no one is there to meet him. David, who is only "between eight and nine" years old, worries if he has been deliberately deserted. But some time later, a gaunt and shabby young man (Mr. Mell), one of the school's masters, calls for him. After David buys something to eat, they go to an alms-house (a poor house) where the schoolmaster visits his poverty-stricken mother.

This short visit over, they complete the journey to Salem House, David's new school. It is a dilapidated old structure with "ink splashed about it" and a general odor of decay. David is admitted by a brutish man with a wooden leg; then he learns that he has been sent to school early as a punishment because the other boys are home for the holidays. He reads the names of the students carved on an old door in the schoolyard and speculates on what they will be like.

A month passes before David is introduced to the sadistic Mr. Creakle, a former hop-dealer and now the proprietor of Salem House. He is a balding man who can only whisper when he speaks and is usually accompanied by the man with the wooden leg, acting "with his strong voice, as Mr. Creakle's interpreter to the boys." Mr. Creakle pinches David's ear, calls him the "young gentleman whose teeth are to be filed" (because of a misunderstanding, he believes that David bites other people), and informs David that he has "the happiness of knowing" David's stepfather.

Mr. Sharp, another schoolmaster and superior to Mr. Mell, returns the next morning, along with Tommy Traddles, a boy whose name David had read carved on the playground door. David is made fun of by the other boys as they arrive, but it is not as bad as he had expected, due largely to Traddles' help. David meets J. Steerforth, one of the senior boys and the acknowledged student leader, who states that David's punishment is a "jolly shame." Steerforth and David are in the same dormitory, and they become friends, primarily because David allows Steerforth to keep his money for him. Steerforth buys some wine and biscuits for them out of the money, and they dine on them as a treat in the evening. The other boys attend the "royal spread," and David enjoys talking about the school with them.

Commentary

David's naiveté at the inn, in Chapter 5, is the first of many similar experiences which he will encounter in the world outside of Blunderstone Rookery. He becomes the butt of jokes both during the journey and at the school. He is homesick for Peggotty and his mother, and on his trip from Yarmouth, he observes children in the

tty takes David to his mother's room to see her

ral, Miss Murdstone gives Peggotty a month's
t David will not be returning to school. David's
e is almost ignored by the Murdstones, and once
isit in the kitchen with Peggotty. She tells him
to Yarmouth to live, and that perhaps (the
ing), David can come and stay with her for a
on is given by Miss Murdstone, and at the end
calls to take them on a journey.

ride, during which Barkis quizzes Peggotty
," they arrive in Yarmouth and are welcomed
gotty. On the way, Peggotty tells David that
Barkis unless "my Davy . . . [is] . . . any-
vid says that he is happy for her.

much the same as David remembers, although
n more beautiful and has become the family
ty inquires about Steerforth, and David
scription of Steerforth's noble character while
tently. David prays that evening that he
rry little Em'ly."

kis courts Peggotty by calling at the house
ntly in the parlour while Peggotty sews. One
d of his visit, David, little Em'ly, Peggotty,
holiday trip together. Mr. Barkis stops the
e and Peggotty go inside. Alone with Em'ly,
e for her, and Em'ly allows him to kiss her.
s from the church, David learns that Mr.
ve just been married.

Murdstones and is neglected again. Most
ading or daydreaming, with an occasional
mily doctor who presided at David's birth.
eek to see David, and on one trip, she indi-
"something of a miser."

one tells David that educating him serves
eeds is a fight with the world—and "the
Mr. Quinion, the manager of Murdstone
ts, has been summoned to escort David to
rk to provide his "eating, drinking, and

streets and wonders "whether their fathers were alive, and whether they were happy at home." David himself is unhappy and he looks forward to the opening of school with apprehension.

In Chapter 6, we are concerned with Steerforth's leadership—a quality implied in his name; his suave manner so impresses the naive David that he is unable to see that Steerforth is using David's money to feed the entire "bedroom." A foreshadowing of future action in this chapter occurs when Steerforth asks David if he has a sister, stating that if David has one, he would like to know her. Although David has no sister, we think of little Em'ly, who is very much like David, and we should remember that Steerforth has complimented David on the very qualities that he and Em'ly share.

CHAPTERS 7-8

Summary

Mr. Creakle opens school the next day by switching a good number of the boys, including David, with a cane; "Half the establishment was writhing and crying before the day's work began," Dickens comments. The beatings are David's most vivid recollection of the school, along with the abuse suffered by poor Traddles who was "caned every day that half-year. . . ."

The classes themselves are conducted within an atmosphere of noise and "sheer cruelty" in which boys are "too much troubled and knocked about to learn." One day the usually gentle Mr. Mell (to whom David is sympathetic) is conducting class and calls for silence in the room, particularly from Steerforth.

Steerforth begins to insult the schoolmaster, calling him a "beggar" and encouraging the other students to join the abuse. Mr. Creakle enters the room and takes Steerforth's side, adding further insult to the poor teacher. Steerforth tells everyone that Mr. Mell's mother is boarded in an alms-house (information which David had innocently told his friend). After further harassment, Mr. Creakle fires the schoolmaster on the spot.

One day, Mr. Peggotty and Ham visit David, bringing him an assortment of seafood and information about the health of the Peggotty household. David asks about little Em'ly, whom Mr. Peggotty describes as "getting to be a woman." Steerforth appears, and Mr. Peggotty and Ham invite him to visit them if he should ever come to Yarmouth.

The half-year passes, with summer days changing to frosty fall mornings, and David looks forward to the holidays when he can return home. Finally school is out, and David begins the long coach trip home to see his mother.

David spends the first night of his return journey at an inn in Yarmouth, where Mr. Barkis calls for him the next morning in his carrier. David tells the driver that he sent Peggotty the message that was requested, but Mr. Barkis replies that "nothing come of it." He asks David to repeat the message to her and to say that he is "a-waiting for an answer." David still does not realize that this is a marriage proposal.

When David arrives home, he finds his mother in the parlor. He is surprised to find her holding an infant, which she introduces as his new brother.

The Murdstones being out on a visit, Peggotty, David, and his mother have supper together and spend a happy evening. David relates Barkis's message again and learns its meaning for the first time.

David's mother implores Peggotty to stay with her, and Peggotty vows that she will. David notices his mother's failing health—"her hand . . . so thin and white"—and her changed manner, "anxious and fluttered." But the familiar scene lulls away his anxiety, and he launches into stories about all that has happened.

The Murdstones return late that evening, and in the morning David apologizes to his stepfather for having been so disrespectful as to bite his hand during their last meeting. Later, however, David is set upon by Miss Murdstone for picking up his baby brother, and his mother is reprimanded for comparing the appearance of her two boys. David feels that he makes everyone, even his mother, uncomfortable with his presence, so he begins spending his evenings with Peggotty in the kitchen. However, he is told sternly "not to associate with servants" and not to retreat to his room during the day. In this way the holidays "lagged away," and David is not sorry when it is time to leave again for school. He will never see his mother again.

Commentary

Chapter 7 further delineates the character of Steerforth, whom David admires, but who, in reality, is a rogue who uses other people

for his own ends. Da
much afraid of his la
forth will bring ab
polished, and hands
people. Ham and N
cultured gentleman
proves to be the m

The wretchedn
is Dickens' protest
tended Wellington
a disguised accou

In Chapter 8
deeply torn betw
her, and his ter
completely domi
that she ends u
Peggotty. Dav
mother cannot
slowly develop

Summary

David's
March, and
ticipating a
prietor's wi
with sincer
by night-co
to return"

David
three dau
David is
funeral a
mother's

Peg
house, v
Murdst
Murdst

the funeral, Peggo
laid out.

After the fune
notice and hints th
presence in the hou
more he is able to v
that she will retur
Murdstones approv
short time. Permiss
of the month, Barki

After a bumpy
about her "situation
by Ham and Mr. Pe
she intends to marry
ways against it." Da

The household is
little Em'ly has grow
favorite. Mr. Peggo
launches into a long de
little Em'ly listens i
"might grow up to ma

Each evening Bar
with a gift and sits sile
day, just before the en
and Mr. Barkis take a
coach at a church, and h
David professes his lov
When the couple returr
Barkis and Peggotty ha

David returns to th
of his days are spent re
visit to Mr. Chillip, the fa
Peggotty comes once a w
cates that Mr. Barkis is

One day, Mr. Murds
no purpose; what David
sooner . . . the better."
and Grinby, wine merchan
London, where he will wo

pocket-money." David realizes that the Murdstones simply want to get rid of him.

Commentary

The sentimentality of Chapter 9 is partially balanced by the realistic psychological behavior of David, who, finding that he is the center of attention by his schoolmates on that last day, makes the most of it and receives a "kind of satisfaction" which makes him feel very "distinguished." This is parallelled by the attitude of Mr. Omer's daughter and her boyfriend, who, although surrounded by a coffin, mourning clothes, etc., continue their courtship, oblivious of the surroundings. Life continues, Dickens seems to say in this chapter; people seek enjoyment even in the face of unhappiness.

In Chapter 10, David's association with the Peggotty household is strengthened, suggesting a continuing relationship. His glowing account of the virtues of Steerforth suggests that he too will be heard of again, and little Em'ly's wide-eyed interest in David's eulogy hints at future developments.

The description of David's life after his return to the Murdstones is one of Dickens' classic themes—*the cruel neglect of children*—worse, in his own view, than physical abuse. "What would I have given to have been sent to the hardest school that ever was kept!" says David.

CHAPTERS 11-12

Summary

Murdstone and Grinby's warehouse is on a wharf; the entire building is overrun with rats and "discoloured with the dirt and smoke of a hundred years." David's job, along with three or four other boys his age, is to wash bottles and paste on new labels. David is introduced to Mr. Micawber, with whom he is to live, and then he is put to work. At eight o'clock, Mr. Micawber returns to take David to his lodgings, where the young lad is introduced to Mrs. Micawber and her small children.

David learns that the family has been forced to take in a lodger because of Mr. Micawber's debts, and later David notices that creditors appear at the house at all hours of the day. However, Mr.

Micawber, with his implicit faith that "something will turn up," seems unperturbed by their demands for money.

David offers to help the family with the loan of his wages, but instead, Mrs. Micawber asks him to pawn household goods for them so that the family can buy food. This suffices for awhile, but at last Mr. Micawber is arrested and taken to debtors' prison, where his family soon joins him; here David observes that "they live more comfortably . . . than they had lived for a long while . . . ." (English jails at that time allowed family members to live with the imprisoned debtor.)

David rents a small room near the prison and continues his solitary existence. The work at Murdstone and Grinby's warehouse is degrading, and the other boys employed there are a lowly group of urchins.

Mr. Micawber holds a dinner party at the prison in celebration of his impending release, and Mrs. Micawber vows to David that she "will never desert Mr. Micawber" no matter how difficult things become. Upon his release, the Micawbers decide to move to Plymouth, where Mr. Micawber can "exert his talents in the country." This influences David to end his "weary days at Murdstone and Grinby's" and run away to Miss Betsey Trotwood, his only relation and a person who he thinks might be sympathetic to his plight.

David writes Peggotty for Miss Betsey's address and the loan of a half-guinea for travelling expenses. When this arrives, he hires a young man with a cart to transport his trunk to the coach office, but the stranger steals his half-guinea and rides off with the trunk. David is alone in London without luggage or funds.

Commentary

Dickens' own childhood forms a good deal of the background of Chapter 11, and Mr. Micawber is a brilliant caricature of Dickens' father. The degradation that David feels at Murdstone and Grinby's is an exact account of the author's feelings about his early life. At the age of nine, Dickens' father, along with the rest of his family, was sent to debtors' prison and Charles became an apprentice in a blacking factory, pasting labels on bottles. His parents appeared to show little concern for Charles' situation, especially the boy's education. Although the Micawbers are treated humorously in the novel, Dickens never forgave his own parents and always thought that his upbringing was no better than an orphan's.

streets and wonders "whether their fathers were alive, and whether they were happy at home." David himself is unhappy and he looks forward to the opening of school with apprehension.

In Chapter 6, we are concerned with Steerforth's leadership—a quality implied in his name; his suave manner so impresses the naive David that he is unable to see that Steerforth is using David's money to feed the entire "bedroom." A foreshadowing of future action in this chapter occurs when Steerforth asks David if he has a sister, stating that if David has one, he would like to know her. Although David has no sister, we think of little Em'ly, who is very much like David, and we should remember that Steerforth has complimented David on the very qualities that he and Em'ly share.

CHAPTERS 7-8

Summary

Mr. Creakle opens school the next day by switching a good number of the boys, including David, with a cane; "Half the establishment was writhing and crying before the day's work began," Dickens comments. The beatings are David's most vivid recollection of the school, along with the abuse suffered by poor Traddles who was "caned every day that half-year. . . ."

The classes themselves are conducted within an atmosphere of noise and "sheer cruelty" in which boys are "too much troubled and knocked about to learn." One day the usually gentle Mr. Mell (to whom David is sympathetic) is conducting class and calls for silence in the room, particularly from Steerforth.

Steerforth begins to insult the schoolmaster, calling him a "beggar" and encouraging the other students to join the abuse. Mr. Creakle enters the room and takes Steerforth's side, adding further insult to the poor teacher. Steerforth tells everyone that Mr. Mell's mother is boarded in an alms-house (information which David had innocently told his friend). After further harassment, Mr. Creakle fires the schoolmaster on the spot.

One day, Mr. Peggotty and Ham visit David, bringing him an assortment of seafood and information about the health of the Peggotty household. David asks about little Em'ly, whom Mr. Peggotty describes as "getting to be a woman." Steerforth appears, and Mr. Peggotty and Ham invite him to visit them if he should ever come to Yarmouth.

The half-year passes, with summer days changing to frosty fall mornings, and David looks forward to the holidays when he can return home. Finally school is out, and David begins the long coach trip home to see his mother.

David spends the first night of his return journey at an inn in Yarmouth, where Mr. Barkis calls for him the next morning in his carrier. David tells the driver that he sent Peggotty the message that was requested, but Mr. Barkis replies that "nothing come of it." He asks David to repeat the message to her and to say that he is "a-waiting for an answer." David still does not realize that this is a marriage proposal.

When David arrives home, he finds his mother in the parlor. He is surprised to find her holding an infant, which she introduces as his new brother.

The Murdstones being out on a visit, Peggotty, David, and his mother have supper together and spend a happy evening. David relates Barkis's message again and learns its meaning for the first time.

David's mother implores Peggotty to stay with her, and Peggotty vows that she will. David notices his mother's failing health—"her hand . . . so thin and white"—and her changed manner, "anxious and fluttered." But the familiar scene lulls away his anxiety, and he launches into stories about all that has happened.

The Murdstones return late that evening, and in the morning David apologizes to his stepfather for having been so disrespectful as to bite his hand during their last meeting. Later, however, David is set upon by Miss Murdstone for picking up his baby brother, and his mother is reprimanded for comparing the appearance of her two boys. David feels that he makes everyone, even his mother, uncomfortable with his presence, so he begins spending his evenings with Peggotty in the kitchen. However, he is told sternly "not to associate with servants" and not to retreat to his room during the day. In this way the holidays "lagged away," and David is not sorry when it is time to leave again for school. He will never see his mother again.

Commentary

Chapter 7 further delineates the character of Steerforth, whom David admires, but who, in reality, is a rogue who uses other people for his own ends. David does not tell him about Em'ly, being "too much afraid of his laughing at me"; yet they will meet and Steerforth will bring about her destruction. Steerforth's superficial, polished, and handsome appearance are weapons which he uses on people. Ham and Mr. Peggotty, like David, believe that he is a cultured gentleman. The unlucky Traddles, in all his misfortune, proves to be the most humane of all the boys.

The wretchedness of the school headed by the cruel Mr. Creakle is Dickens' protest against many schools of that period. Dickens attended Wellington Academy in North London, and this is probably a disguised account of his own schooling.

In Chapter 8, the main emphasis is on the fact that David is deeply torn between his love for his mother and the desire to be near her, and his terrible dislike for the Murdstones. The Murdstones completely dominate David's mother and have such control over her that she ends up defending the Murdstones in an argument with Peggotty. David's realization that the gulf between him and his mother cannot be bridged under these conditions is a stage in his slowly developing maturity.

CHAPTERS 9-10

Summary

David's tenth birthday falls on a foggy school day during March, and he is called into Mr. Creakle's parlour, happily anticipating a basket from Peggotty. Instead he is told by the proprietor's wife that his mother has died. "If ever child were stricken with sincere grief, I was," says David, as he prepares to return home by night-coach the next afternoon, not imagining that he is "never to return" to Salem House.

David is met in Yarmouth by Mr. Omer who, along with his three daughters, makes a living preparing funeral arrangements. David is fitted for a funeral suit, and over tea he learns from the funeral arranger that his infant brother has also died and "is in his mother's arms."

Peggotty meets David at the door and ushers him into a silent house, where even the Murdstones don't speak to one another. Miss Murdstone sits imperturbably at her desk each day, writing; Mr. Murdstone alternately sits and paces silently. A day or two before the funeral, Peggotty takes David to his mother's room to see her laid out.

After the funeral, Miss Murdstone gives Peggotty a month's notice and hints that David will not be returning to school. David's presence in the house is almost ignored by the Murdstones, and once more he is able to visit in the kitchen with Peggotty. She tells him that she will return to Yarmouth to live, and that perhaps (the Murdstones approving), David can come and stay with her for a short time. Permission is given by Miss Murdstone, and at the end of the month, Barkis calls to take them on a journey.

After a bumpy ride, during which Barkis quizzes Peggotty about her "situation," they arrive in Yarmouth and are welcomed by Ham and Mr. Peggotty. On the way, Peggotty tells David that she intends to marry Barkis unless "my Davy . . . [is] . . . anyways against it." David says that he is happy for her.

The household is much the same as David remembers, although little Em'ly has grown more beautiful and has become the family favorite. Mr. Peggotty inquires about Steerforth, and David launches into a long description of Steerforth's noble character while little Em'ly listens intently. David prays that evening that he "might grow up to marry little Em'ly."

Each evening Barkis courts Peggotty by calling at the house with a gift and sits silently in the parlour while Peggotty sews. One day, just before the end of his visit, David, little Em'ly, Peggotty, and Mr. Barkis take a holiday trip together. Mr. Barkis stops the coach at a church, and he and Peggotty go inside. Alone with Em'ly, David professes his love for her, and Em'ly allows him to kiss her. When the couple returns from the church, David learns that Mr. Barkis and Peggotty have just been married.

David returns to the Murdstones and is neglected again. Most of his days are spent reading or daydreaming, with an occasional visit to Mr. Chillip, the family doctor who presided at David's birth. Peggotty comes once a week to see David, and on one trip, she indicates that Mr. Barkis is "something of a miser."

One day, Mr. Murdstone tells David that educating him serves no purpose; what David needs is a fight with the world—and "the sooner . . . the better." Mr. Quinion, the manager of Murdstone and Grinby, wine merchants, has been summoned to escort David to London, where he will work to provide his "eating, drinking, and pocket-money." David realizes that the Murdstones simply want to get rid of him.

Commentary

The sentimentality of Chapter 9 is partially balanced by the realistic psychological behavior of David, who, finding that he is the center of attention by his schoolmates on that last day, makes the most of it and receives a "kind of satisfaction" which makes him feel very "distinguished." This is parallelled by the attitude of Mr. Omer's daughter and her boyfriend, who, although surrounded by a coffin, mourning clothes, etc., continue their courtship, oblivious of the surroundings. Life continues, Dickens seems to say in this chapter; people seek enjoyment even in the face of unhappiness.

In Chapter 10, David's association with the Peggotty household is strengthened, suggesting a continuing relationship. His glowing account of the virtues of Steerforth suggests that he too will be heard of again, and little Em'ly's wide-eyed interest in David's eulogy hints at future developments.

The description of David's life after his return to the Murdstones is one of Dickens' classic themes—*the cruel neglect of children*—worse, in his own view, than physical abuse. "What would I have given to have been sent to the hardest school that ever was kept!" says David.

CHAPTERS 11-12

Summary

Murdstone and Grinby's warehouse is on a wharf; the entire building is overrun with rats and "discoloured with the dirt and smoke of a hundred years." David's job, along with three or four other boys his age, is to wash bottles and paste on new labels. David is introduced to Mr. Micawber, with whom he is to live, and then he is put to work. At eight o'clock, Mr. Micawber returns to take David to his lodgings, where the young lad is introduced to Mrs. Micawber and her small children.

David learns that the family has been forced to take in a lodger because of Mr. Micawber's debts, and later David notices that creditors appear at the house at all hours of the day. However, Mr.

Micawber, with his implicit faith that "something will turn up," seems unperturbed by their demands for money.

David offers to help the family with the loan of his wages, but instead, Mrs. Micawber asks him to pawn household goods for them so that the family can buy food. This suffices for awhile, but at last Mr. Micawber is arrested and taken to debtors' prison, where his family soon joins him; here David observes that "they live more comfortably . . . than they had lived for a long while . . . ." (English jails at that time allowed family members to live with the imprisoned debtor.)

David rents a small room near the prison and continues his solitary existence. The work at Murdstone and Grinby's warehouse is degrading, and the other boys employed there are a lowly group of urchins.

Mr. Micawber holds a dinner party at the prison in celebration of his impending release, and Mrs. Micawber vows to David that she "will never desert Mr. Micawber" no matter how difficult things become. Upon his release, the Micawbers decide to move to Plymouth, where Mr. Micawber can "exert his talents in the country." This influences David to end his "weary days at Murdstone and Grinby's" and run away to Miss Betsey Trotwood, his only relation and a person who he thinks might be sympathetic to his plight.

David writes Peggotty for Miss Betsey's address and the loan of a half-guinea for travelling expenses. When this arrives, he hires a young man with a cart to transport his trunk to the coach office, but the stranger steals his half-guinea and rides off with the trunk. David is alone in London without luggage or funds.

Commentary

Dickens' own childhood forms a good deal of the background of Chapter 11, and Mr. Micawber is a brilliant caricature of Dickens' father. The degradation that David feels at Murdstone and Grinby's is an exact account of the author's feelings about his early life. At the age of nine, Dickens' father, along with the rest of his family, was sent to debtors' prison and Charles became an apprentice in a blacking factory, pasting labels on bottles. His parents appeared to show little concern for Charles' situation, especially the boy's education. Although the Micawbers are treated humorously in the novel, Dickens never forgave his own parents and always thought that his upbringing was no better than an orphan's.

Chapter 12 develops the characters of the Micawbers, who were introduced in the previous chapter as David's landlords. The mutual good feeling between David and the family suggests that their relationship will ripen into deep friendship.

In addition, David's escape from drudgery leads him into deeper troubles as he sets out for Miss Betsey's. This is an example of Dickens' protest against the exposure of children to hardships, a protest that is found in so much of his writing.

CHAPTERS 13-14

Summary

Determined to reach Miss Betsey's home in Dover, David sets out on foot. He passes a small second-hand clothing store, sells his waistcoat for a small sum, and then spends the night in a haystack near Salem House School.

David, "a dusty, sunburnt, half-clothed figure," arrives in Dover after six days of traveling and inquires about his aunt. After several unsuccessful inquiries, he is directed to Miss Trotwood's cottage. Miss Trotwood, seeing the ragged urchin in her garden, sternly bids him, "Go away! Go along! No boys here!" But when David tells her who he is and what an unhappy life he has led since his mother's death, she takes charge of him with vigor, but it should be added, with abruptness.

Janet, the Trotwood housekeeper, is directed to prepare a bath for David; in the meantime, his aunt feeds him some broth. After David naps, he is fed a large supper while Miss Trotwood comments on the folly of marriage. The conversation is interrupted with her cry, "Janet! Donkeys!" Suddenly Miss Trotwood and the housekeeper rush outside to chase the donkey-riders off the lawn. This is a frequent occurrence at the cottage.

The household consists of Miss Trotwood, the housekeeper, and Mr. Dick, a congenial simpleton whom Miss Trotwood has befriended. They are all kindly people, and David feels fortunate to be there.

At breakfast the next morning, Miss Trotwood tells David that she has written to his stepfather. David implores her not to send him back, but she is noncommittal in her reply.

David visits with Mr. Dick (actually, his name is Mr. Richard Babley, but he detests the name), who is writing a long "Memorial" to the Lord Chancellor. When a part of the manuscript is finished, Mr. Dick uses it to paper a huge kite. In this way Mr. Dick circulates his "facts a long way." David thinks him quite mad, but a harmless, friendly fellow nonetheless.

A reply to Miss Trotwood's letter arrives, stating that the Murdstones are coming to speak to her about David. David is terrified at the prospect of this visit. When the Murdstones arrive the next day, they immediately incur the wrath of Miss Trotwood by guiding their donkeys across the front lawn. Finally, the Murdstones enter the house, and David's stepfather tells about the many difficulties he has had with the rebellious boy. Miss Trotwood counters by saying that David's interests, particularly his annuity, has not been looked after and that his mother was ill-used. Exasperated, Mr. Murdstone states that if David does not return, "my doors are shut against him. . . ."

Miss Trotwood asks David if he wishes to return, and he replies that he does not; she then asks Mr. Dick what she should do with the boy and after a bit of thought, he replies, "Have him measured for a suit of clothes directly." She thanks Mr. Dick for his good sense, and with some final caustic remarks, she ushers the Murdstones out of the house. David now has a new set of guardians and his aunt decrees that he shall now be known as "Trotwood Cooperfield." And so David begins a new life.

Commentary

In Chapter 13, Dickens uses elements of the popular picaresque, or adventure story. This type of novel was well established in Dickens' time and consisted of the wandering journey of a hero through a series of thrilling, unconnected incidents. The hero is forced to live by his wits as he encounters different people (usually of low station) who attempt to cheat him or otherwise use him for their own ends. Because the hero sees all levels of society, the author is able to give a panoramic picture of life during a particular time.

The delineation of Miss Trotwood's true character in Chapter 14 is Dickens' way of revealing that behind the brusque exterior shown in the first chapter lies a compassionate nature. Note, too, her concern, as evidenced in her guardianship of Mr. Dick and her instinctive rejection of the Murdstones.

CHAPTERS 15-16

Summary

It is decided that David will attend school in Canterbury, and the next day Miss Trotwood escorts David on his journey. In Canterbury they stop at the office of Mr. Wickfield, a lawyer, and are welcomed at the door by a Mr. Uriah Heep, a red-haired clerk about fifteen years old. Miss Trotwood has come for advice on which school to enroll David in. Mr. Wickfield takes Miss Trotwood to visit "the best we have," while David observes Uriah Heep, whose eyes look "like two red suns."

Miss Trotwood likes the school, but none of the available boarding houses suit her, so it is decided that David will board with Mr. Wickfield. David meets Mr. Wickfield's daughter, Agnes, a girl of David's age, and he is then shown his room. David's aunt tells him to "be a credit to yourself, to me, and Mr. Dick," embraces him, and then departs.

After supper that evening, David notices that Mr. Wickfield drinks a great deal of wine. Just before bedtime, David sees Uriah Heep closing up the office, and after a brief conversation, David says goodnight and shakes Uriah's hand. "But oh, what a clammy hand his was! as ghostly to the touch as to the sight. I rubbed mine afterwards, to warm it, *and to rub his off.*"

David begins school the next day and is introduced to his new schoolmaster, Doctor Strong, a carelessly dressed man with a "lustreless eye," whose life's project is the writing of an immense never-to-be-completed dictionary. With Dr. Strong is his pretty wife, Annie, who is much younger than her husband. In a conversation between Wickfield and Strong, David hears about one of Annie's cousins, a Mr. Jack Maldon, apparently a loafer, for whom Mr. Wickfield is trying to find some suitable provision.

Although school is very pleasant, it has been so long since David has mingled with boys his own age that he is apprehensive about how he will get on with his classmates. He has such an initial fear of his new situation that he hurries back to Mr. Wickfield's at the close of the first day of classes to avoid meeting any of the students.

After dinner that evening, Mr. Wickfield has his usual large portion of wine. David enjoys Agnes' company; however, he reassures himself that he loves Em'ly—but yet he feels "there are goodness, peace, and truth, wherever Agnes is."

When it is time for bed, David notices Uriah Heep is still in the office, poring over a huge book. Heep is studying law, but he contends that he is far too "umble" ever to become Mr. Wickfield's partner. Instead, Uriah suggests that David might "come into the business," but David protests that he has "no views of that sort."

David learns more about Doctor Strong from some of the boys that board at his house. The old Doctor has been married to the pretty young Annie for less than a year, and during that time he has had to support a host of her relatives. Among them is Mrs. Markleham (known to the boys as the Old Soldier), who is Annie Strong's mother.

One night, a small party is held for Jack Maldon, who is leaving for India "as a cadet, or something of that kind, Mr. Wickfield having at length arranged the business." It is also Doctor Strong's birthday. Mrs. Markleham, in wishing him "many, many, many happy returns," thanks him for what he has done for her family, but she does it in such a way that her self-centeredness is clearly revealed. She also mentions that she remembers when Jack Maldon was "a little creature, a head shorter than Master Copperfield, making baby love to Annie. . . ."

Throughout the evening, Mrs. Strong seems ill at ease. Although she is "a very pretty singer," she is unable to begin a duet with her cousin, Jack Maldon, and when she tries to sing by herself, her voice dies away and she is left "with her head hanging down over the keys."

As Maldon departs, David notices that he is carrying "something cherry-coloured in his hand." Shortly afterward, Annie is found in a swoon, and her mother notices that her bow, a "cherry-coloured ribbon," is missing. Annie says that she thinks she had it safe, a little while ago.

Commentary

In Chapter 15, we first meet one of the notable villains of all of English literature—Uriah Heep. His future activities will play an important part in the lives of several of the characters. As yet he is only a boy, and it is doubtful that his ambitions are formed, although they are perhaps already in the making. Dickens has managed to make Uriah Heep so unpleasant physically that he is repulsive to David.

Although Mr. Wickfield is obviously a good man, we should already detect a weakness in his character—if only in the fact that he feels that he has to drink a great quantity of wine each night before going to bed. He is devoted to his daughter, whom he calls his "little housekeeper," and she is equally devoted to him.

We see in Chapter 16 that after an initial period of adjustment, David is happy in Doctor Strong's school, and he has every reason to be. It is "an excellent school, as different from Mr. Creakle's as good is from evil." There is "an appeal, in everything, to the honour and good faith of the boys," and the boys feel that they have "a part in the management of the place, and in sustaining its character and dignity." Such a school was virtually unknown in Dickens' day, indicating that he had educational views that were *far ahead* of their time.

CHAPTERS 17-18

Summary

David, in corresponding with Peggotty, returns the half guinea she loaned him, and he learns from her that the Murdstones have moved from the house in Blunderstone, leaving it "shut up, to be let or sold."

At school, David is visited, occasionally, by his aunt and also by Mr. Dick on alternate Wednesdays. On one of Mr. Dick's visits, he tells David about a strange man who has been hanging around the Trotwood house frightening Aunt Betsey and causing her to faint. Unaccountably, Mr. Dick has seen her give *money* to the strange man.

Uriah Heep asks David to have tea with him and his mother, if their "umbleness" doesn't prevent him. David accepts the invitation, and that evening he meets Mrs. Heep, "the dead image of Uriah, only short." Although there has been a considerable lapse of time since Mr. Heep's death, Mrs. Heep is still wearing "weeds" (black mourning dresses).

Mrs. Heep and her son proceed to "worm things out" of David, first about his past life, and then about Mr. Wickfield and Agnes. David has begun to feel "a little uncomfortable" and to wish himself "well out of the visit," when Mr. Micawber suddenly appears. He has been walking down the street and through the open door, he spied David. David introduces Micawber to Uriah and his mother.

The next evening, David looks out of the windows and is surprised to see Mr. Micawber and Uriah Heep "walk past, arm in arm." He learns, the next day when he dines with the Micawbers, that Mr. Micawber went home with Uriah and drank brandy and water at Mrs. Heep's. Micawber is much impressed with Uriah and says that if he had known him when his "difficulties came to a crisis . . . my creditors would have been a great deal better managed" than they were.

The next morning, David receives a note from Mr. Micawber saying that there is no hope of receiving the money from London, and indicating that Micawber will soon be returning to debtors' prison. David, on his way to school, hurries toward the hotel "to soothe Mr. Micawber with a word of comfort." However, he meets "the London coach with Mr. and Mrs. Micawber up behind, Mr. Micawber the very picture of tranquil enjoyment." David is both relieved and sorry at their going.

David reminisces about his school days. He remembers being in love with Miss Shepherd, "a little girl . . . with a round face and curly flaxen hair," and how "all was over" when she made a face and laughed at him one day. He also remembers the boys at Doctor Strong's school and how the Doctor "waylaid the smaller boys to punch their unprotected heads.'

In time, David becomes the head-boy at the school, and he feels that the boy he was when he first came to the school is no longer part of him. "That boy is gone"; also gone is the little girl he "saw on that first day at Mr. Wickfield's. . . . In her stead, the perfect likeness of [her mother's] picture—a child-likeness no more—moves about the house, and Agnes . . . is quite a woman."

Again David is in love, this time with Miss Larkins, a woman of about thirty. Although she has many officers as admirers, David dreams of winning her. He dances with her at a ball, and for several days afterward, he is lost "in rapturous reflections." One day Agnes tells him that Miss Larkins is to be married to an elderly hop-grower, Mr. Chestle. David is "terribly dejected for about a week or two." He is now seventeen.

Commentary

In Chapter 17, we have the first of several far-fetched *coincidences* that appear in the novel. The possibility of Mr. Micawber's just happening by at a time when David is an awkward position, and wishes to escape, is very remote. It may be argued that such things *do* indeed happen now and then in real life, but they happen so rarely that when a coincidence is used in a novel—just to further the plot—it does seem artificial, especially to today's readers.

Also artificial (for today's readers) is Dickens' use of a *mysterious stranger*, whose identity is not revealed for some time (although it is not impossible to guess at once who he is). The stranger was used by Dickens to heighten reader interest and to add an element of suspense to the story; the novel, remember, was originally published in serial form and many of the conventions that you are reading here were original with Dickens and were borrowed by many lesser and later writers.

With Chapter 18, we are now at the end of what many readers believe is the finest part of the novel—David's childhood and school days. We have watched him grow from babyhood to the age of seventeen, and he has become, through Dickens' great sympathy for him, a truly believable character. In fact, David may well be the only *truly* believable character in the novel; most of the others merely possess exaggerations of the traits we meet every day.

CHAPTERS 19-20

Summary

Unsure of what he wishes to do in the world, David is encouraged by Aunt Betsey to visit Peggotty so that he may have "a little change" and "thereby form a cooler judgment." His aunt gives him a "handsome purse of money, and a portmanteau" (a suitcase), and he sets out.

David first stops at Canterbury to say goodbye to Agnes and Mr. Wickfield. While he is there, Agnes tells David that she is worried about her father's condition. David says that he has become concerned over Mr. Wickfield's increased drinking, that whenever Mr. Wickfield "is least like himself," he is most certain to be wanted on "some business" by Uriah Heep.

Later at Dr. Strong's, David observes another domestic problem. A letter has arrived from Jack Maldon in which he states that he is ill and wants to return. Mrs. Markleham succeeds in getting Dr. Strong to let Maldon come over while Annie "never once spoke or lifted up her eyes." David senses trouble ahead.

Arriving in London, David registers at a hotel and is given a small room over a stable. After a dinner during which he tries to give an impression of worldly maturity, he attends a performance of *Julius Caesar* at Covent Garden. When he returns to the hotel, he is overjoyed to run into James Steerforth, now an Oxford student; he is on his way home to visit his mother. Steerforth admonishes one of the hotel's employees for giving David such a poor room, and David is immediately given a much better room.

The next morning at breakfast, Steerforth invites David to come home with him and meet his mother. David accepts the invitation, and at dusk they arrive by stagecoach at an old brick house in Highgate, a suburb of London. Steerforth's mother is elderly and rather formal. Her companion is Rosa Dartle, a thin, black-haired lady of about thirty. Miss Dartle has a scar on her lip, which Steerforth tells David he caused. "I was a young boy, and she exasperated me, and I threw a hammer at her."

David invites Steerforth to go with him to visit the Peggotty family, and Steerforth is interested but condescending. He expresses pleasure at the chance "to see that sort of people"; he tells Miss Dartle that "there's a pretty wide separation between them and us. . . . They are wonderfully virtuous, I dare say. . . . But they have not very fine natures, and they may be thankful that, like their coarse rough skins, they are not easily wounded."

Commentary

Throughout Chapter 19, we see David trying to find his place in a mature world—adopting manners which he associates with maturity but which seem rather amusing to the reader. David is finding it hard to assert himself, and it is easier for him to stand by quietly rather than risk taking a stand that might expose his immaturity. In contrast, Steerforth is a man of the world. He demands what he wants when he wants it. And he is imperious enough to get it.

Jack Maldon's imminent return from India suggests that an interesting subplot is building up in the Strong household. As yet it is not clear just what feelings may remain from childhood days, when Annie was Maldon's sweetheart.

In Chapter 20, during the time that David spends with the Steerforth family, Dickens' main emphasis is on the intense love that Mrs. Steerforth feels for her son. He is the very center of her existence, and she no doubt values anything if it has a relationship to her son. For example, it is obvious to us that her *only* interest in David is the fact that he, too, is devoted to Steerforth.

Of interest in this chapter, also, is Rosa Dartle; she has a peculiar, indirect way of seeking information from others, hinting rather than speaking outright. Steerforth sums her up nicely: "She brings everything to a grindstone and sharpens it, as she has sharpened her own face and figure these years past. . . . She is all edge."

CHAPTERS 21-22

Summary

During his stay at the Steerforth home, David is much impressed with Littimer, a servant there. "He surrounded himself with an atmosphere of respectability, and walked secure in it. It would have been next to impossible to suspect him of anything wrong, he was so thoroughly respectable," David says of Littimer.

Finally, David and Steerforth leave for Yarmouth and, arriving late, spend the night at an inn. The next morning, David goes alone to visit Mr. Barkis and Peggotty. On the way he comes to Mr. Omer's shop, which is now listed as OMER AND JORAM. David goes inside and talks to Mr. Omer, who tells him that Little Em'ly works in his shop as a seamstress and that she mixes well with the other girls—apparently because of her rare beauty and her dream of becoming a "lady."

David calls on Peggotty, who at first fails to recognize him. She takes David upstairs to see Mr. Barkis, now a rheumatic invalid confined to bed. Steerforth arrives a little later, and after dinner, he and David set out for the Peggotty houseboat. As they walk along the shore, Steerforth comments that "the sea roars as if it were hungry" for them.

They arrive just as the engagement between little Em'ly and Ham is being announced. The family is overjoyed, and the jubilant

Mr. Peggotty exclaims that "no wrong can touch my Em'ly." David and Steerforth are welcomed into the celebration, and when Steerforth leaves the Peggotty home, he remarks that Ham is "rather a chuckle-headed fellow for the girl, isn't he?" David feels a shock in this unexpected and cold comment. But, "seeing a laugh in his eyes," he thinks that Steerforth must be joking. "Ah, Steerforth! . . . When I see how perfectly you understand them . . . I know that there is not a joy or sorrow, not an emotion, of such people that can be indifferent to you."

Steerforth replies, "I believe you are in earnest, and are good. I wish we all were!"

During the visit, which lasts for more than two weeks, Steerforth spends a great deal of time boating with Mr. Peggotty, while David visits his old home at Blunderstone. The old neighbors have moved and his parents' graves have been cared for by Peggotty; David feels "a singular jumble of sadness and pleasure" about his early years here.

One evening, David is surprised to find Steerforth in a despondent mood. He does not tell David what is bothering him, but says only that he wishes "with all my soul I could guide myself better." The mood is only momentary, however, and he soon improves his spirits and tells David that he has bought a used boat, renaming it the *Little Em'ly*. Mr. Peggotty will be the "captain" in Steerforth's absence. David believes this to be evidence of his friend's charity toward Mr. Peggotty.

Later, Steerforth's austere and respectable servant, Littimer, arrives with a letter from Steerforth's mother. Then there is another arrival—Miss Mowcher, a fat, middle-aged dwarf, who is a hairdresser for wealthy families. Steerforth describes Little Em'ly to the dwarf as "The prettiest and most engaging little fairy in the world. . . . I swear she was born to be a lady."

Later, David walks back to the Barkis house and finds Ham waiting outside for Em'ly. She is in the house talking to Martha Endell, a girl who once worked with her at Mr. Omer's. Ham explains to David that Martha Endell is a "fallen woman," and because Mr. Peggotty would not want Em'ly to speak to her, she earlier gave the girl a note telling her to meet her at the Barkis cottage. Ham gives Martha some money so that she can go to London, where she is not known. After Martha leaves, little Em'ly sobs, "I am not as good a girl as I ought to be! Not near! Not near!"

Commentary

Sometimes Dickens' chapters tend to ramble; this is not the case, however, with Chapter 21. Here, he pulls together two strands of David's story—his old friends at Yarmouth and his old school friend Steerforth. Dickens takes the opportunity here to point up the *simple goodness* of the Yarmouth people, and he once again hints at character flaws in Steerforth.

Chapter 22, in contrast to Chapter 21, is more ambiguous. Although it is not explicitly stated, there seems to be an indication that little Em'ly has entered upon a secret relationship with Steerforth. Steerforth shows some remorse over his behavior, as evidenced by his brooding, but it is short-lived. Em'ly, perhaps seeing in the fate of Martha Endell something of her own possible fate, sobs as Martha leaves. She tells Ham, "Oh, my dear, it might have been a better fortune for you if you had been fond of someone else—of someone steadier and much worthier than me."

There is also an interesting new facet of Steerforth revealed in this chapter when Steerforth tells David that it might have been better for him (Steerforth) if he "had had a steadfast and judicious father." We have seen in Chapter 20 the excessively motherly devotion that Mrs. Steerforth has lavished upon her son; thus, by now, we should be beginning to suspect that Steerforth is *not* the paragon that everyone in the story believes him to be.

CHAPTERS 23-24

Summary

Steerforth and David depart by coach the next morning, leaving Littimer behind to do "what he has to do," as Steerforth cryptically comments. During the journey, David tells Steerforth about the previous night's encounter with Martha Endell, the "fallen woman." David seeks Steerforth's advice about which profession he should pursue. He inquires about being a proctor, a job suggested to him in a recent letter from his aunt, but Steerforth comments that it is a dull job; David would be "a sort of monkish attorney at Doctors' Commons."

David meets Aunt Betsey in London and tells her that he would be happy to be a proctor. However, when he learns that it will cost his aunt a thousand pounds to place him with a firm, David asks if she can afford it. Her reply is that she has "*no* other claim upon my means—and you are my adopted child."

The next day they set out for the office of Messrs. Spenlow and Jorkins, in Doctors' Commons, where David is to learn his new profession. On the way, an "ill-dressed man" approaches them, and for a moment Aunt Betsey is terrified. However, to David's great astonishment, she tells him to wait for her, and she drives off in a coach with the strange man. When Aunt Betsey returns a half hour later, she tells David, "Never ask me what it was, and don't refer to it." Significantly, David notices that all the guineas are gone from her purse when she gives it to him to pay the driver of the coach.

At the law office, David meets Mr. Spenlow, a well-dressed little man, who explains that his partner, Mr. Jorkins, is a ruthless taskmaster (Later David finds him to be a mild man and learns that his image as a tyrant is a ruse to pressure people). Arrangements are made for David to begin a month's probation, and after everything is arranged, David is lodged at the home of Mrs. Crupp, who immediately takes a motherly interest in him. The next day his aunt leaves for Dover, and David is ready to begin his career in law.

At first David is pleased with his living quarters, but he soon becomes lonely and wonders why Steerforth has not come to visit. When Steerforth turns up, David invites him and two of his Oxford friends to dinner, and he tries to arrange with Mrs. Crupp to cook the meal. However, Mrs. Crupp is unable to prepare the food, and it must be ordered from the pastry cook.

During dinner, everyone consumes a great deal of wine, and David soon becomes "singularly cheerful and light-hearted" and even tries smoking for the first time. It is suggested that they attend the theater, and on the way out, David is conscious of someone falling down the stairs. He is surprised to find that it is he.

The theater is very hot, and to David "the whole building looked . . . as if it were learning to swim." They go downstairs to where the ladies were; there, the boisterous David becomes the center of attention. He discovers Agnes at the theater with some friends and tries to talk to her. She is embarrassed and asks him to leave. Steerforth helps David return home. The next morning David is plagued with remorse and shame—and with a headache.

Commentary

In Chapter 23, David is launched on a career through his aunt's benevolence. But a disturbing element in her life (a life seemingly so mysteriously free of any past) is introduced, suggesting that there is something or someone in her past to account for the belligerent, withdrawn character we first knew her as. For example, we should ask ourselves at this point: who is the mysterious stranger who so greatly terrifies Aunt Betsey?

Chapter 24 is one of Dickens' most entertaining chapters in this novel. Young David's becoming intoxicated and making a fool of himself is underplayed just enough to make the scene realistic yet comic. His attempts to talk to Agnes and his abrupt "Goori" (goodnight) when he is told to leave, are examples of classic Dickens humor.

CHAPTERS 25-26

Summary

Two mornings after the dinner party, just as David is about to leave his room, a messenger arrives with a letter from Agnes, asking him to meet her at the home of Mr. Waterbrook, her father's London agent. When David meets Agnes, he reproaches himself for his conduct at the theatre. Agnes is forgiving, and David calls her his "good Angel." She warns David against Steerforth, his "bad Angel," but David insists that Steerforth is a good and loyal friend.

Agnes then relates her growing fears about Uriah Heep, who seems to be gaining more and more power over her father. In fact, Agnes believes that Uriah is going to enter the firm as a partner. David is indignant about this and tells Agnes that she must prevent it. Agnes, however, asks David to be congenial to Uriah for her father's sake.

The next day David attends a dinner party at Mr. Waterbrook's and encounters Uriah Heep again. While David is with Agnes, he senses Uriah's "shadowless eyes and cadaverous face, to be looking gauntly down . . . from behind." David is pleased to find Tommy Traddles, his old schoolmate, at the party. He learns that Traddles is preparing for the bar and, at the same time, working for the pompous Mr. Waterbrook. After the party, David suddenly remembers

Agnes' plea to be kind to Uriah Heep, and so he invites him to his room for coffee. There, Uriah reveals his increasing sense of power and even confides that he loves Agnes and hopes to marry her. David is appalled at this prospect. Uriah asks if he can spend the night, and in the morning, after Uriah leaves, David asks Mrs. Crupp to "leave the windows open, that my sitting-room might be aired and purged" of his presence.

When Agnes leaves to return to Canterbury, Uriah Heep appears and boards the same coach. David is uneasy and fears that Uriah may succeed in his desire to marry Agnes. In addition, Steerforth is now at Oxford, and although letters pass between them, David remembers Agnes' warning and harbors "some lurking distrust" of him.

David begins his apprenticeship with the firm of Spenlow and Jorkins. One day, Mr. Spenlow invites David to come for a visit to his house at Norwood to meet his daughter, who has been attending school in Paris. When Mr. Spenlow and David arrive at the house, David is introduced to Dora Spenlow and is immediately overcome with her loveliness. "All was over in a moment. I had fulfilled my destiny. I was a captive and a slave. I loved Dora Spenlow to distraction!"

David is understandably startled to find Miss Murdstone at the Spenlow home; she is serving as a hired companion and protecter for Dora. David at first fears that Miss Murdstone will disparage him to Dora, but he and Miss Murdstone, when they are alone, agree to keep their past relationship a secret. David learns that Dora does not like Miss Murdstone; her closest friend is her dog, Jip.

Back in London, David lives in a dream about Dora and buys sumptuous waistcoats, "not for myself; *I* had no pride in them, for Dora."

Commentary

Chapter 25 is important primarily because it introduces Agnes Wickfield; she is the first person in the book to sense the true character of Steerforth. Everyone else, including David, has been dazzled by his charms. However, Dickens has already suggested to the *reader* that Steerforth's seeming perfection hides weak self-indulgence (for which his mother is largely responsible). We suspect that he is furthering an interest in little Em'ly, despite her engagement to Ham.

When Dickens relates the discussion at the dinner party in this chapter, note how carefully he portrays the shallowness of human feeling as he describes the "upper classes." Here, the conversation centers around the "terribly" great importance of "blood"—meaning that only families of the aristocracy are of any concern.

David's feelings for Dora, in contrast, are handled realistically; in fact, most critics believe that they are based on Dickens' own life. When Dickens was about eighteen, he fell in love with Maria Beadnell, but her father sent her away to Paris so that she could not see the young suitor and Dickens saw very little of her after that.

CHAPTERS 27-28

Summary

David goes to visit Tommy Traddles, who lives in a very poor section of Camden Town, where garbage and junk clutter the streets. David finds Traddles' apartment house, whose "genteel air" reminds him of the days he spent with Mr. and Mrs. Micawber. They discuss their school days and Traddles' life since leaving school. He explains to David that he went to his uncle's household to live, but his uncle didn't like him. After his uncle's death, Traddles began to copy law writings for a living and then to "state cases" and make abstracts. This led him to the study of law, which exhausted his limited funds. He then found jobs with a couple of other offices, including Mr. Waterbrook's, as well as with a firm that was preparing to publish an encyclopaedia. Finally, he "managed to scrape up" the hundred pounds necessary for him to be "articled." Traddles also reveals that he is engaged to be married to one of the ten daughters of a curate in Devonshire. He expects it to be a long engagement, but they have made a beginning by buying two small pieces of furniture.

David is surprised and delighted to learn that Traddles' landlord is Mr. Micawber, who is still patiently waiting for something to turn up. David talks with Mr. and Mrs. Micawber and learns that they are expecting another child. He is invited to dinner but declines the invitation; instead, he asks them to dine with him at a later date.

David makes arrangements about the dinner party which he plans for the Micawbers and Tommy Traddles, but he has to compromise with Mrs. Crupp by agreeing to eat out for the next two weeks; otherwise, she will not cook the meal. When his guests arrive, Mr. Micawber becomes involved in preparing the punch, while Mrs. Micawber sits at the dressing table and gets herself ready for the party.

As they all sit around eating the mutton, Littimer arrives and asks David if he has seen Steerforth. When David says that he hasn't, Littimer says that Steerforth will probably be coming up from Oxford tomorrow. He insists that David be seated, and he then takes over the task of preparing the remainder of the mutton. During Littimer's presence, everyone is uncomfortable, and it is only when the servant leaves that they seem "to breathe more freely." Before Littimer goes, David asks him if he remained long at Yarmouth. Littimer says that he stayed to see the boat completed but he does not know if Steerforth has seen it yet.

The conversation turns to Mr. Micawber's employment. It is agreed that the corn business, in which Micawber is employed, is not very profitable and that Mr. Micawber should advertise his talents in the papers—"throw down the gauntlet" to society, as it were—to see what will turn up. The cost of this advertising will be met by a promissory note. Before the party adjourns, David warns Traddles not to act as co-signer for any bills, but Traddles says that he has already done so.

Shortly afterward, Steerforth appears. David, as a result of Agnes' warning, has been feeling a slight uneasiness about him. However, he is now so overjoyed at seeing his friend that he feels "confounded and ashamed" at having doubted him. Steerforth has just come from Yarmouth, and he gives David a letter from Peggotty, which says that Barkis is gravely ill. David decides to visit Peggotty, but Steerforth persuades David to spend the next day with him at his home before going to Yarmouth.

Commentary

In the opening of Chapter 27, David is reminded of the Micawbers. This may lead readers familiar with Dickens to believe that, before the chapter ends, Mr. Micawber will put in an appearance. Dickens does not disappoint these readers. This is another unlikely *coincidence*, but something one has to understand is part of Dickens' technique, just as was his having Miss Murdstone show up in Chapter 26, as an employee in the Spenlow household. The possibility of this happening in real life is very remote, but it helped lace together Dickens' intricate network of plots and subplots.

When we get to Chapter 28, we see that David has matured from the time he first knew Mr. Micawber, and he now realizes that his old friend is a failure. This is clearly shown when he warns Traddles not to co-sign any bill with Micawber.

Steerforth, while discussing the approaching death of Barkis, reveals a ruthlessness in his nature. "It's a bad job . . . but the sun sets every day, and people die every minute, and we mustn't be scared by the common lot. No! Ride on! Roughshod if need be, smooth-shod if that will do, but ride on! Ride over all obstacles and win the race!"

David shows the first indication of his having matured in regard to Steerforth when, after leaving him, he remembers what his friend said about riding over *all* obstacles and winning the race. David finds himself wishing, for the first time, that Steerforth "had some worthy race to run."

CHAPTERS 29-30

Summary

David is cordially received at the Steerforth residence, especially by Rosa Dartle, who begins asking him questions about Steerforth's activities. She blames David for keeping Steerforth away from home longer than usual, and she hints that something may cause a quarrel between Steerforth and his mother.

Steerforth flatters Miss Dartle into playing the harp and singing for them, and David comments that her song is the most "unearthly" he has ever heard. When Miss Dartle finishes playing, Steerforth laughingly puts his arm around her and says, "Come, Rosa, for the future we will love each other very much!" Miss Dartle promptly strikes him and angrily leaves the room. David asks why she did this, but Steerforth says he does not know, but that she is "always dangerous."

Before retiring for bed, Steerforth tells David that should something ever separate them, "think of me at my best." Before leaving the next morning, David looks in at Steerforth sleeping peacefully in his bed. In retrospect, he realizes he would never see Steerforth again as a friend. "Never more, oh God forgive you, Steerforth! to touch that passive hand in love and friendship. Never, never more!"

David arrives in Yarmouth and takes a room in the village inn because he feels that the spare room at Peggotty's is probably taken by "the great Visitor—Death." He meets Mr. Omer in his shop and is told that Mr. Barkis is dying. He inquires about Em'ly, and Mr. Omer says that she has become "unsettled" recently and that he will be relieved when she's married. Word arrives that Barkis is unconscious and beyond help, and David rushes to the house.

At the house, everyone thanks David for being kind enough to come. Em'ly appears and seems shaken and chilled; she turns away from Ham to cling to Mr. Peggotty. Mr. Peggotty explains that it is her youth which causes her to take the dying of Barkis so hard; however, David is puzzled by her actions. David is then taken in to see Barkis, who is propped up and just barely conscious. Peggotty assures David that he will not die until the tide is out (an old superstition of English fishermen). Barkis opens his eyes for the last time and sees David. With a pleasant smile he says, "Barkis is willin' " and goes "out with the tide."

Commentary

It is obvious in Chapter 29 that Rosa Dartle is in love with Steerforth, despite the fact that she is some years older than he. But it is a neurotic sort of love, mixed with much bitterness and perhaps even hatred. It is doubtful that such a woman could love openly, for she has hidden her emotions behind an attempt to be self-effacing; furthermore, she resents all that stands between her and Steerforth —his mother, even Steerforth himself, and, more recently, David. Steerforth, of course, probably has never known for sure of Miss Dartle's love for him, but he has, of course, sensed it, and he has idly played with it in his self-indulgent way.

Miss Dartle, in implying that something may come between Steerforth and his mother, has shrewdly guessed that Steerforth is involved in some possible scandal. But she does not know any details. She believes that David does and she questions him, but he knows nothing, as yet, about Steerforth's secret activities.

By the time we finish Chapter 30, we are almost half-way through the novel. Dickens has introduced scores of characters, major and minor. With the death of Barkis we begin to see how Dickens disposes of them—to clear the way for further development, to provide drama and pathos, and to pick up loose ends.

CHAPTERS 31-32

Summary

David is entrusted with the will of the deceased Mr. Barkis, and he prides himself on his ability to read the document and distribute the items in the proper manner. David has found the will in the mysterious box which Barkis carried with him religiously all these years. Along with the will, the box contains "miniature cups and saucers, a horseshoe, a polished oyster shell . . . and almost three thousand pounds." Peggotty is provided for in the will, as is Mr. Peggotty, with David and Em'ly as minor heirs.

Only Peggotty, Mr. Peggotty, and David attend the funeral. That evening David goes to Mr. Peggotty's houseboat. Everyone tries to cheer up Peggotty by telling her that she did her "dooty by the departed, and the departed know'd it." Mr. Peggotty lights the candle for Em'ly (as he has done for so many years) and places it in the window. He vows that even after Em'ly is married he will continue to put the candle in the window, "pretending I'm expecting of her, like I'm a-doing now." Ham arrives at the house, but without Em'ly. He draws David, alone, out of the house and weeps as he tells him that Em'ly has run away with her lover. The others, too, learn of the situation, and David reads to them a farewell note she left for Ham. Mr. Peggotty asks who the man is, and Ham cries, "Mas'r Davy, it ain't no fault of yourn—and I am far from laying of it to you—but his name is Steerforth, and he's a damned villain."

Mr. Peggotty announces, "I'm a-going to find my poor niece in her shame, and bring her back. No one stop me! I tell you I'm a-going to seek my niece!" Mrs. Gummidge collects her wits, stops feeling sorry for herself, and, for the first time, takes a mature, forceful interest in handling affairs by talking Mr. Peggotty out of leaving the house that very night. David hears him crying and tells us that "I cried too."

Even though Steerforth has run off with Em'ly, David still thinks of all the favorable things about him; he chooses to think of Steerforth as "a cherished friend, who was dead." Late one night, David is interrupted by the unexpected visit of a tearful and agitated Miss Mowcher, who reveals her part in the plot. She had been tricked into sending communications between Em'ly and Steerforth through Littimer. Now, "suspecting something wrong," she has returned from London. Miss Mowcher believes that Em'ly and Steerforth have gone abroad and vows revenge. "Littimer had better have a bloodhound at his back than little Mowcher," she vows.

The next morning, Mr. Peggotty, Peggotty, and David leave for London, where they decide to visit Mrs. Steerforth. Mrs. Steerforth is quite unmoved by Em'ly's letter and her wish to return a "lady." She states emphatically that her son's marriage to Em'ly is "impossible." If Steerforth returns without Em'ly, she will forgive him; otherwise "he never shall come near me."

Mr. Peggotty takes a little money from his sister to begin his search. "If any hurt should come to me, remember that the last word I left for her was, 'My unchanged love is with my darling child, and I forgive her!' "

Commentary

Clearly in Chapter 31, David's maturity is becoming more and more evident. In the simple matter of the reading of the will, David feels "supreme satisfaction" that he is the only one able to do this. Yet, at the end of the chapter, he weeps because, for the first time, he is fully aware of the evil nature of the clever Steerforth.

The death of Barkis in the preceding chapter was handled with restraint, but with this "greater loss," Dickens pulls out all the stops with his description of the night, the rain, and the feelings of the family as they realize that Em'ly is gone. This is the climax of the Em'ly-Steerforth plot, or subplot.

Chapter 32 is yet one more example of Dickens' depicting the upper classes as heartless and cruel. The forgiving nature of Mr. Peggotty is diametrically opposed to the cold aloofness at the

Steerforth house, where Miss Dartle calls the Peggotty group a "depraved, worthless set." Dickens, probably because of his upbringing, felt that only "simple people" had the capacity to feel deeply and to be sentimental about things.

CHAPTERS 33-34

Summary

David reveals how much he loves Dora Spenlow; thoughts of her continually enter his mind and he despises any man who does not realize how wonderful Dora is. In the meantime, he manages Peggotty's affairs, "proving the will" and putting all her business in an orderly fashion. After the legal matters are settled, David takes Peggotty to the "Commons office" to pay her bill and is startled to meet Mr. Murdstone in Mr. Spenlow's company. The conversation between Mr. Murdstone, David, and Peggotty is very strained, as David still remembers the heartaches this man caused. Mr. Murdstone is in the law office to obtain a marriage license so that he can wed a girl who has just come of age.

David and Mr. Spenlow go into court to settle a divorce case and afterwards they engage in a lengthy conversation about the law. David feels that many aspects of the law are in need of reform and suggests some changes in the workings at the law office, but the conservative Mr. Spenlow considers it "the principle of a gentleman to take things as he found them." Mr. Spenlow forgets about his personal reform movement.

On the day of the picnic David hires a "gallant grey" horse, buys a bouquet of flowers, and rides to the Spenlow home. Dora is in the garden with a friend, Miss Julia Mills, and with Jip, her dog. They all leave for the picnic, and David stares at the beautiful Dora the entire trip. He is so absorbed that he is surprised to find other people are at the picnic too. His jealousy is aroused by a red-whiskered gentleman who competes with him throughout the day for Dora's company, and David tries his best to forget his feelings by flirting with another girl at the celebration and even contemplates leaving. As the picnic ends, Julia Mills tells David that Dora will be staying at her home for a few days, and she invites him to come to call on them. David is elated once more.

Three days after the picnic, David goes to visit Dora; he plans to declare his great passion for her. After much timidness, he finally bursts forth with his feelings and they become engaged, but they decide to keep the betrothal a secret for the time being. David, however, goes to a jeweler and buys a ring to seal the engagement. Within a week, they have their first quarrel, but Miss Mills is able to bring the couple back together.

David writes to Agnes informing her of his engagement to Dora and about the circumstances of Em'ly's flight. He is anxious to impress Agnes with his sincere love for Dora. Traddles comes up to David's room, and they exchange conversation about their fiancées before Traddles asks a favor of David. He explains that Mr. Micawber is still having financial problems and, consequently, has changed his name to Mr. Mortimer, has taken to wearing glasses, and only goes out at night in order to avoid his creditors. Traddles adds that he has signed his name for only one of Mr. Micawber's recent debts. His own difficulty is that he has had some of his personal possessions seized by the pawnbroker who lent money to Mr. Micawber; now the pawnbroker raises the prices whenever Traddles attempts to buy them back. Peggotty and David buy back Traddles' things and return to David's apartment. There, they find visitors: Aunt Betsey is sitting on her luggage and Mr. Dick is holding a huge kite. His aunt tells him that she has lost all her wealth and is ruined. "All I have in the world is in this room, except the cottage," she says, and *that* must be put up for rent. The old lady is undaunted, however, and she reminds David that "We must meet reverses boldly, and not suffer them to frighten us. . . . We must live misfortune down."

Commentary

Early in his life, Dickens worked as a lawyer's clerk and then as a parliamentary reporter for a newspaper. Here in Chapter 33, he trades in on that experience to flesh out the reality of this episode. Through his experiences, he developed a deep suspicion of the law and its workings. In this chapter, more than perhaps anywhere else in the novel, Dickens satirizes governmental officials who have large comfortable offices while whose who do the real work are shut up in cold, dark rooms.

After the critical attack on petty officials in the preceding chapter, Dickens turns to a warmer tone in Chapter 34. Aunt Betsey, who was once David's sole means of support, is the focus here; she is financially unable to provide for herself now and must even stay the night with David in order to save expenses. David is called upon to be "firm and self-reliant" so that he can help the person who befriended him when *he* was in trouble. David's maturity soon will stand its greatest test.

CHAPTERS 35-36

Summary

After David gets his aunt settled, he has a long discussion with Mr. Dick about her poverty. When Mr. Dick begins to cry, David has to cheer him up. Peggotty and Mr. Dick then leave for the night, and David and his aunt talk about Dora, his new-found love. Miss Trotwood implies that the girl is "light-headed" and "silly"; however, she does not interfere with the relationship. She then expresses her approval of Peggotty (she renames her "Barkis") even though "the . . . ridiculous creature . . . has been begging and praying about handing over some of her money" to Miss Trotwood. Finally David and his aunt retire, but David is too upset to sleep well. He has continuous dreams of poverty the rest of the night.

The next morning, David goes to the law office of Spenlow and Jorkins to "cancel his articles" and recover a portion of his aunt's thousand pounds which had been put up for his tuition. He is refused, however, and is forced to return home empty-handed. As David leaves the law office, he meets Agnes Wickfield, who is on her way to see Miss Trotwood. Agnes has come to London with her father and Uriah Heep, and she tells David that Mr. Heep (and his mother) live with them now and that Uriah has become a full partner in the firm, exerting an overpowering influence on her father.

David and Agnes return to the house and surprise Miss Trotwood. She is very happy to see Agnes and tells them both how she came to lose her fortune: Agnes' father had taken care of her money and all her affairs, but after he teamed up with Uriah Heep, she decided to invest the money herself, "and a very bad market it turned out to be." Agnes tries to help by suggesting that David can find extra work as a secretary to Dr. Strong; without hesitation, David resolves to see Dr. Strong about the position.

In high spirits, David sets out to prove himself worthy of his aunt's faith and Dora's love. He goes to Highgate to see Dr. Strong and succeeds in gaining part-time employment. The arrangement stipulates that David must work every morning and every evening, five days a week for seventy pounds a year, allowing him to pursue his studies for the rest of the day. The primary drawback of this job is the necessity of overcoming the "efforts" of Jack Maldon, who has returned from India and has been "helping" the doctor; for example, he complicated one of the doctor's manuscripts by making numerous mistakes and obscuring it with various sketches.

Impatient to do even more odd jobs, David goes to see Traddles. His purpose is to inquire about earning more money by reporting the debates in Parliament for a newspaper. Even though Traddles tells him about the extreme difficulty of mastering "the mystery of shorthand writing and reading," David decides to start work on it immediately. Next, Mr. Dick's problem is considered. Upset by Miss Trotwood's reverses, Mr. Dick constantly frets about having nothing useful to do. His dilemma prompts Traddles to find him work copying legal documents. The first week's earnings for this work give Mr. Dick such joy and satisfaction that he confides to David that he is *sure* that he will be able to provide for Miss Trotwood.

Traddles, excited by Mr. Dick's success, nearly forgets about a letter which Mr. Micawber sent to David by him. In the letter which Mr. Micawber has sent, he tells of his intention of moving away to accept another position and he invites his two friends to a small celebration on the eve of the departure. Arriving at the Micawbers, David learns that "the Micawbers are going to Canterbury, where Mr. Micawber is to be the confidential clerk of Uriah Heep!"

Commentary

In Chapter 35, Dickens reveals to us that Miss Betsey has reservations about David's sweetheart, Dora. She feels that David needs someone to "sustain him and improve him," and she chides him that, when it comes to love, he is "blind, blind, blind." Agnes acts as a captive audience for David's recital of his love for Dora. At the end of the chapter, as David leaves for his rooms, he hears a blind beggar call "Blind! Blind! Blind!" and it reminds him (and us) of what his aunt has said.

David's sudden acceptance of new responsibilities and his extreme determination to prove his worth highlight Chapter 36. His determination to master shorthand so that he can report debates in Parliament is partially boyish enthusiasm (it will take several years of study), the rest resolution "to turn the painful discipline of my younger days to account, by going to work with a resolute and steady heart." Further evidence of David's maturity is evident if he is compared to other characters who, although older than he, do not have such a determined and levelheaded approach.

CHAPTERS 37-38

Summary

Mrs. Crupp attempts to intimidate Miss Trotwood as she tried to intimidate Peggotty but David's Aunt Betsey proves too strong a character for her, and David observes that Mrs. Crupp "subsided into her own kitchen, under the impression that my aunt was mad." David is very comfortable in his aunt's care.

Although David loves Dora, he has not told her about his being poor and he decides that he must. At first, she refuses to understand and then she begins to cry. David tries to explain that he deeply loves her, but she tells him, "Don't talk about being poor, and working hard." She is more concerned about whether or not her dog, Jip, will have a daily mutton-chop! David explains that it would help if Dora would try to learn something about housekeeping and cooking, but this causes Dora to become almost hysterical and she faints. Finally, Miss Mills enters the room and calms Dora. Later Miss Mills tells David that Dora "is a favorite child of nature" and that practical responsibilities are beyond her scope.

David discovers that learning shorthand is very difficult, but because he is stimulated by his love for Dora and aided by Traddles' advice and assistance, he becomes rather confident of his skill. Finally, David experiments by trying to record one of the speakers in the Commons. Unfortunately, he discovers that he needs much more practice.

Going to the Commons one day, David is called into the upstairs room of a neighboring coffeehouse by Mr. Spenlow, Dora's

52

father; there, he is confronted by Miss Murdstone, holding all of his letters to Dora. It seems that Dora's dog, Jip, was playing with one of the letters and Miss Murdstone found it. Mr. Spenlow is *very* angry, and when David states that he and Dora are engaged, Mr. Spenlow is determined to protect his daughter from the "consequences of any foolish step in the way of marriage," even to the extent of threatening to change his will if necessary. Mr. Spenlow says that he will forget the matter if David, in turn, will forget about marrying Dora. When David refuses, Mr. Spenlow gives him a week to reconsider, and if David decides not to, he will send Dora abroad again.

During the week, David consults Miss Mills, but this only makes him feel more miserable and depressed than before.

The next Saturday, David appears at the Commons and learns that Mr. Spenlow died mysteriously the night before. A few days later, Mr. Jorkins, David, and an office clerk search Mr. Spenlow's desk for a will, but none is found; rather, it is discovered that his records are out of order, that he has lived beyond his income, and that Dora will be left with very little money. She is sent to live with two maiden aunts, and the only news David hears of her is by way of a journal kept by Miss Mills, his "sole companion of this period."

Commentary

Chapter 37 deals foremost with the matter of David's being deeply in love and not quite comprehending what *we* clearly see: Dora, in her present state, will prove little more than a hindrance to him. He would be far better off with the sisterly Agnes.

The key episode in Chapter 38 parallels Dickens' own love affair with Maria Beadnell. Mr. Spenlow hints that Dora might be shipped off to Paris to prevent her marriage; Mr. Beadnell did that very thing. In the novel, Mr. Spenlow dies, and David is able to marry his sweetheart, but in real life Dickens was not so fortunate to have had this happen.

CHAPTERS 39-40

Summary

Aunt Betsey sends David to Dover to supervise the renting of her cottage, the only possession she has left; she hopes that this responsibility will lift David out of his depression.

David rapidly concludes the business in Dover and continues on to Canterbury to visit Mr. Wickfield and Agnes. At Mr. Wickfield's house, David talks to Mr. Micawber (now Uriah's clerk) about his new job. David finds that Mr. Micawber is pleased with his new employer and thinks that his work is a "great pursuit." David, however, senses an "uneasy change" in him.

David talks to Agnes about his troubles and how much he misses her advice on matters. He says that he finds it difficult to confide in Dora in the same way because she is so "easily disturbed and frightened." Agnes suggests to David that he write to Dora's aunts and seek permission to visit Dora.

After leaving Agnes, David goes downstairs to see Uriah Heep and Mr. Wickfield. Mrs. Heep is also living there, and David thinks of the Heeps as "two great bats hanging over the whole house and darkening it with their ugly forms." Next day, David takes a walk. He is followed by Uriah, who confides that he fears that David might be a rival for Agnes. David reluctantly tells Uriah that he is "engaged to another young lady," which obviously relieves Uriah. Reassured, Uriah tells David about his education in the London charity schools, where he learned to eat "umble pie with an appetite." Now Uriah is proud to note that he has "a little power."

At dinner, David sees Uriah use this power by suggesting that he hopes to marry Agnes. Mr. Wickfield becomes furious, and David tries to calm him. Uriah becomes frightened that Mr. Wickfield, in his anger, will "say something . . . he'll be sorry to have said afterwards," and tries to return to his "umbleness" again. Wickfield expresses to David his shame over his downward path in life and slowly starts to sob. Agnes comes in and comforts her father, and they leave the room together. Later that night David makes her promise that she will "never sacrifice herself" for a "mistaken sense of duty." Next morning, as David leaves, Uriah admits that perhaps he has "plucked a pear before it was ripe." But, says the sinister Uriah, "It'll ripen yet! I can wait!"

One snowy night, on his way home from Dr. Strong's, David passes a woman on the street whom he recognizes but cannot recall; seconds later, as he meets Mr. Peggotty, he realizes the woman whom he passed was none other than Martha Endell, the "fallen woman" whom Em'ly had once helped. The chance meeting with

Mr. Peggotty takes place on the steps of St. Martin's Church, on a route David took only because of the storm.

Mr. Peggotty shows David various letters which he received from Em'ly, in which she asks for understanding and forgiveness, and indicating clearly that she will never return. The letters also contain money, obviously originating from Steerforth, but Mr. Peggotty vows that he will return every cent of the money if he has to go "ten thousand miles." The last note received bears the postmark of a town on the Upper Rhine, and Mr. Peggotty declares that he is going there now in search of Em'ly. Throughout Mr. Peggotty's story, David sees Martha Endell listening at the inn door. After awhile they part, and the grieving uncle "resumes his solitary journey."

Commentary

Finally in Chapter 39 Uriah Heep is beginning to show his true colors. His protestations of "umbleness" are now as many as ever, but his account of his early days in the charity school reveals that his "false humility" is an educated policy rather than his personal philosophy. Heep has Mr. Wickfield in his control and intends to keep secret the source of his control.

The pathetic journey in Chapter 40 of the good and noble Mr. Peggotty was the type of scene which Victorian readers loved. Undaunted by hardships, getting along the best way he can, the loving "father" seeks his wayward child to the far corners of the earth. Martha Endell, the tainted symbolic "sister," will be instrumental in saving Em'ly just as she is about to become a prostitute. In this chapter, Dickens once again uses *coincidence* (fortuitous meetings) to further the intricacies of plot and subplot.

CHAPTERS 41-42

Summary

David receives a reply to his letter to Dora's aunts, Miss Lavinia and Miss Clarissa Spenlow, stating that he may call upon them—accompanied by a "confidential friend" if they so desire. David asks Traddles to go with him, and during the trip Traddles passes the time with the story of his own engagement to Sophy and the objections he encountered from her family. This makes David even more nervous.

The Spenlow sisters are dressed in black and remind David of two birds, "having a sharp, brisk, sudden manner . . . like canaries." David's anxiety is not helped when they address Traddles as Mr. Copperfield. As the conversation advances, David finds that the decision about David's courtship will be made by Miss Lavinia, the younger of the two sisters. After a period of questioning, answering and lecturing, it is decided that David "may court" Dora.

In time, Aunt Betsey becomes acquainted with the Spenlows, and everyone adjusts quite well to the circumstances, except Jip, the dog. David notices that the aunts treat Dora like a child; however, when he mentions this to Dora, she starts to cry, so he drops the subject. He also attempts to teach Dora something about becoming a housewife; he brings her a "cookery book" and begins to instruct her on how to keep account books. Dora soon becomes disgusted when the columns do not add up for her and she starts to draw pictures all over the books. David does not make any progress and decides just to enjoy her company.

After Agnes arrives with her father on a visit of a fortnight to the Doctor's, Uriah corners David in the Doctor's garden. He hints that he is in love with Agnes, and then he expresses hatred for Annie, Doctor Strong's young wife, because he feels that she stands between Agnes and him. He goes on to imply a relationship between Annie and Jack Maldon.

On the next evening, David takes Agnes to meet Dora. Since David is anxious that "Agnes should like her," he is pleased to find that they become very friendly. In fact, Dora considers Agnes so clever that she wonders why David fell in love with her rather than with Agnes.

After David leaves Agnes at Dr. Strong's house, he sees a light in the Doctor's study and enters to find Mr. Wickfield, Doctor Strong, and Uriah Heep in a troubled state. Uriah tells David that he has just informed Dr. Strong of the "goings-on" between Annie and Jack Maldon. Mr. Wickfield admits that he himself thought Annie may have married the Doctor for "worldly considerations only." Dr. Strong, however, criticizes himself for the situation because his wife is so much younger than he, and he cannot help but regard Annie as the "wronged" partner.

After the Doctor and Mr. Wickfield leave the room, David argues with Uriah over "entrapping me into your schemes" and becomes so angry that he slaps Uriah on the cheek.

David later notices that the Doctor exhibits a "gentle compassion" toward his wife and urges her to spend more time with her mother, Mrs. Markleham, "to relieve the dull monotony of her life." Annie is unhappy over this estrangement from her husband, and David often notices her "with her eyes full of tears." Only Mr. Dick serves as "a link between them."

David receives a letter from Mrs. Micawber. She says that "Mr. Micawber is entirely changed. . . . He is secret." She tells David that she is having difficulty obtaining even the barest of expense money from him, and she asks for David's advice.

Commentary

In Chapter 41, Dickens gives us another clear picture of Dora, showing her as the shallow, impractical child or "pretty toy," unable to face anything requiring even a slight measure of self-discipline. She is a lovable person, if a simple one; however, the reader can only wonder at David's deep love for her and be dubious about the possibility of success in the marriage now planned.

In Chapter 42, Dickens focuses on yet another woman: the innocent Annie as she is being slandered by Uriah. Here, David comes to the rescue and strikes him, but he is unable to combat the schemes of the villainous clerk. In all of the subplots in the latter part of this long novel, David is merely an observer of the action, for the main part, and is powerless to intercede.

CHAPTERS 43-44

Summary

David reminisces about his life and remembers how his love for Dora continued to grow. He is now twenty-one and has "tamed that savage stenographic mystery [shorthand]" and reports the debates in Parliament for "a morning newspaper." He is also writing for magazines with some success and says, "Altogether, I am well off." His greatest happiness, however, is due to his coming marriage.

Miss Lavinia and Miss Clarissa, Dora's aunts, have given their consent to the marriage and are now in a state of frenzy trying to make the bride's wardrobe. Aunt Betsey helps by hunting for furniture in the London stores while Peggotty cleans and recleans the cottage where David and his new wife will live. Tommy Traddles attends the wedding. Sophy, Traddles' fiancée, and Agnes Wickfield are bridesmaids.

After David reaches the church door, "The rest is all a more or less incoherent dream." However, after the wedding breakfast, David and Dora drive away together, and he awakens from the dream to realize, "It is my dear, dear, little wife beside me, whom I love so well!"

The glamour of the wedding wears off almost at once. Their servant, Mary Anne Paragon, is a poor cook. David tells Dora to talk to her about the preparation of meals, but Dora's only recourse is to cry. David asks his aunt to explain housekeeping to his wife, but she refuses and tells David that he must have patience with "Little Blossom" and to "estimate her . . . by the qualities she has, and not by the qualities she may not have." She goes on to say, "This is marriage, Trot; and Heaven bless you both in it, for a pair of babes in the wood as you are!"

A line of incompetent servants comes and goes at the cottage. When David and Dora go shopping, the merchants cheat them. One night Traddles comes to dinner, but the house is so cluttered that David wonders if there is enough room for Traddles to use his knife and fork. Jip walks on the table, "putting his foot in the salt or the melted butter." The mutton is barely cooked, and the oysters that Dora bought cannot be opened. When Traddles leaves, Dora says she is sorry, but David confesses, "I am as bad as you, love." Later, David is "assisted" in his writing by his "child-wife," who sits beside him and holds the pens while he writes.

Commentary

The first part of Chapter 43 draws upon Dickens' own beginnings as a writer. He became a parliamentary reporter for the *London Morning Chronicle*, and during this time his first articles about London life were published in magazines. Shortly after this, in 1836, he married Catherine Hogarth, although he apparently cared more for Mary Hogarth, his wife's sister. This relationship is somewhat paralleled in *David Copperfield* by that between David and Agnes, whom David loves here as a sister.

Dickens' description of the wedding no doubt pleased Victorian audiences, but his method of presenting it as a mere backward glance severely underplays the action so that the description seems quaint and artificial, like a faded photograph.

Chapter 44 continues with this same sort of autobiographical paralleling. Although the circumstances of David's courtship are based largely on Dickens' involvement with Maria Beadnell, the incompetence of Dora reflects Dickens' attitude toward his own wife, Catherine Hogarth. It is interesting also to note the similarity in the names of Maria Beadnell and Martha Endell, which may indicate another subconscious reference by the author.

CHAPTERS 45-46

Summary

David frequently sees Dr. Strong and observes that his marriage is becoming more troubled. Mrs. Markleham, the "Old Soldier," drags Annie around to operas, concerts, and other forms of entertainment, even though Annie would prefer to stay at home. Although Dr. Strong encourages Annie to get out more, the selfish Mrs. Markleham widens the gap between the couple. Mr. Dick becomes disturbed over this because both Dr. Strong and Annie are his friends. Aunt Betsey, while speaking with David, predicts that Mr. Dick will soon "distinguish himself in some extraordinary manner."

One night Mr. Dick visits David in his parlour. Mr. Dick expresses his concern over the marital drift between the Doctor and his wife. He asks if the Doctor is angry with her, and David replies, "No. Devoted to her." "Then I've got it, boy!" Mr. Dick replies. Then one evening in the autumn, David and his aunt visit Dr. Strong. Mrs. Markleham is at the house and says that she has just overheard the Doctor making out a will in which he leaves everything to Annie. Mrs. Markleham is pleased about this and thinks that it is only right. Everyone goes into the study, where David notices Mr. Dick standing in the shadow of the room. Annie glides into the room "pale and trembling." Mr. Dick supports her on his arm and lays the other hand upon the Doctor's arm. Annie kneels in front of her husband and begs him "to break this long silence." Dr. Strong will only say that it is not her fault. It is left up to David to explain the suspicion that Uriah Heep has aroused in her husband. Annie then dispels the suspicion that she married the Doctor for his money and exposes her *mother* as the opportunist. Annie admits that before she married the Doctor she had liked Jack Maldon "very much . . . very much." She also says that they had been "little lovers once" and that she might have come to "persuade" herself that she really loved him and might have married him and "been most wretched." She then assures her husband, ". . . in my lightest thought I have never wronged you—never wavered in the love and fidelity I owe you!" Afterward, the two are reunited, and after the reunion, Aunt Betsey attributes the success of the affair to Mr. Dick. "You are a very remarkable man, Dick!"

David has been married almost a year and is becoming more and more successful in his writing. One night, as he is walking home and thinking about the novel he is writing, he passes the Steerforth house. He is stopped by Mrs. Steerforth's maid, who tells him that Rosa Dartle wishes to speak with him.

Miss Dartle asks David if Em'ly has been found, and when David answers that he knows nothing about her, Miss Dartle sadistically suggests, "She may be dead." Miss Dartle calls Littimer into the room to give a report. Littimer explains that he and a Mr. James traveled all over Europe with Em'ly and that she was admired wherever they went. He says that Em'ly, however, was often depressed, and that she and Steerforth frequently quarreled until finally Steerforth left her. Before departing, Steerforth implied that she should marry Littimer. Littimer says that Em'ly was so upset that he had to watch her constantly so that she wouldn't kill herself. He then says that Em'ly escaped from him and has not been seen since. Once again Miss Dartle expresses the hope that Em'ly ("this low girl") may be dead.

The next evening, David goes to Hungerford Market in London to find Mr. Peggotty. David informs him of what he has learned from Littimer, and they agree that the best chance of finding Em'ly would be through Martha Endell, Em'ly's friend, who has been living in London; before they leave to find Martha, Mr. Peggotty sets out a candle and also lays out one of Em'ly's dresses. By coincidence, David and Mr. Peggotty come upon Martha and follow her until they reach an appropriate place to talk.

Commentary

Poetic justice takes its turn in Chapter 45. Mrs. Markleham is exposed for the selfish person that she is. The "devoted" Doctor and his unwavering wife are reunited, and one of Dickens' subplots has run its course. Dickens also shows himself to a bit of the "champion of the underdog" in this chapter by allowing the weak-minded Mr. Dick to succeed in reuniting the couple.

Dickens slows his narrative in Chapter 46 by allowing Littimer to comment at length on his travels with Em'ly. He states that she speaks different languages and "wouldn't have been known for the same country person . . . her merits really attracted general notice." However, her greatest pleasures seem to be sitting on the beach and talking to the boatmen's wives and children. David is able to picture her "sitting on the far-off shore, among the children like herself when she was innocent, listening to the little voices such as might have called her Mother had she been a poor man's wife." When Em'ly first met David, she feared the sea and wanted to be a "lady," choosing Steerforth over Ham because Steerforth represented to her a chance of escaping the fishing town and becoming a "lady." This episode foreshadows Em'ly's eventually forsaking her selfish ambitions. The attempt to realize an ambition by selfishly ignoring the feelings of others is, according to Dickens, a tragic character flaw that can only end in unhappiness.

CHAPTERS 47-48

Summary

David and Mr. Peggotty catch up with Martha just as she approaches the bank of a river (probably the Thames). David realizes she is about to commit suicide, and, with the help of Mr. Peggotty, he pulls her back from the edge of the water. Martha begins to sob that it would be best if she jumped in the river because her life is so miserable. Martha blames herself for Em'ly's disappearance and is beside herself with grief because Em'ly had been so kind to her. David explains that she is not to blame and that they are there to ask her to help them find the missing girl. Martha now has a reason to live and vows never to give up until Em'ly is found.

David returns to his aunt's home and observes that the mysterious stranger who had so upset Aunt Betsey is in the garden. His aunt comes out of the house and gives the man some money and the man leaves. David asks his aunt who this man is, and she confides that it is her *husband*. She explains that she has been separated from him for many years and that he has become a gambler and a cheat. She says that she still gives him money out of nostalgia for their past love but that it embarrasses her to have him turn up at her home. She then asks David to keep the subject a secret.

While working for the newspaper, David has managed to complete a novel, which becomes a success. Surprisingly, he is not "stunned by the praise." He does, however, decide to give up reporting.

David has been married for a year and a half, and he and Dora still have little luck with housekeeping. They employ a page, but this man constantly fights with the cook and steals food from them. He finally ends up in jail for stealing Dora's watch. David then decides that he should "form Dora's mind," so she can become more responsible in household management. He begins by reading Shakespeare to her and by giving out "little scraps of useful information, or sound opinion." This fails, and David begins to think about Agnes and to wonder what things would have been like if he hadn't met Dora.

David hopes that their expected baby will change his "child-wife" into a woman, but the baby dies shortly after birth and Dora's health begins to fade. One night Aunt Betsey bids goodnight to "Little Blossom," and David cries to think, ". . . Oh what a fatal name it was, and how the blossom withered in its bloom upon the tree!"

Commentary

Two important themes of Dickens are highlighted in Chapter 47; these are the disciplined heart and wise prudence. Although Dickens has portrayed Aunt Betsey as a woman whom David admires, or whom Dickens himself admires, even *she* has a weakness, for she reveals to David that her husband is still alive, and that it is he to whom she has been giving considerable sums of money. She recalls the time "when she loved him [her husband] . . . right well . . . [but] he repaid her by breaking her fortune and nearly breaking her heart." Yet she still gives him money, "sooner than have him punished for his offences." It is only in Agnes that Dickens comes close to his "perfect" human being. Agnes has both admirable emotional control and the prudence to wait for David, who returns her unexpressed love by loving her as a sister.

Dora's death is clearly foreshadowed in Chapter 48 by David's comparing Dora with a withering blossom. It is also foretold by the condition of Jip, the dog. The dialogue concerning Jip is also indicative of Dora's impending death. Dora comments, "He is getting quite slow," and Aunt Betsey immediately replies, "I suspect . . . he has a worse disorder than that." After the baby dies, Dora becomes so weak that David must carry her up and down the stairs. Clearly we can anticipate another deathbed scene.

CHAPTERS 49-50

Summary

David receives a long, flowery letter addressed to him at Doctors' Commons from Mr. Micawber in which he tells David that he wants to meet with him and Traddles at King's Bench Prison. The letter is perplexing, and David reads it several times to unscramble its meaning.

David and Traddles meet Mr. Micawber at the designated place and they sense that much is on his mind. David asks about Uriah Heep, and Mr. Micawber says that he is sorry for anyone who knows such a man. Finally, they board a coach and go to Aunt Betsey's house, where they can talk. Both Aunt Betsey and Mr. Dick are present. They ask Mr. Micawber to make some of his wonderful punch, but he is so upset that he forgets what he is doing and ruins the drink. Mr. Micawber eventually reveals the name of the person who is the cause of his emotional upset: "Villainy is the matter . . . and the name of the whole atrocious mass is—HEEP!" Mr. Micawber calls him a "detestable serpent" and vows that he will crush the "hypocrite and perjurer." Micawber makes some mention of the Wickfields, but, before explaining what Heep has done to them, he rushes from the house. As he leaves, he mentions a future meeting at which he plans to "expose [this] intolerable ruffian—HEEP!" David later receives a "pastoral note" from Mr. Micawber, asking them to be present at an inn in Canterbury one week from now for this purpose.

David fears that Em'ly must be dead, but Mr. Peggotty still believes that she is safe and will be returned to him. During this time, Mr. Peggotty has been a frequent visitor at David's house, and both Dora and David admire the man for his abiding faith.

One night Martha visits David and tells him they must journey to London immediately; she has left a note for Mr. Peggotty to follow as soon as possible, yet she says nothing of what to expect. When they arrive in London, David is taken to a shabby rooming house where he and Martha observe Rosa Dartle entering Martha's apartment just ahead of them. David and Martha listen through a side door, and David recognizes Em'ly's voice. They hear Miss Dartle blaming Em'ly for Steerforth's going away, as she hurls insults at the poor girl. Em'ly pleads for mercy, but Miss Dartle continues her vindictive abuse. "If you live here tomorrow, I'll have your story and your character proclaimed on the common stair." David is frequently tempted to interrupt the scene, but he decides to wait for Mr. Peggotty.

Miss Dartle hurries out of the room and down the stairs, brushing past the onrushing Mr. Peggotty. Em'ly cries "Uncle" and faints in Mr. Peggotty's arms; he tenderly carries her motionless body down the stairs.

Commentary

In Chapter 49, Dickens turns to autobiography again as he expresses the oratorical mannerisms of his own father in Micawber's penchant for writing flowery letters; also, the childlike impulses that characterized Dickens' father are illustrated in Micawber. He is unwilling to reveal the problem that is causing him so much agony, for example, until he is asked to make his favorite punch and is cajoled into talking by the others.

Chapter 50 is often said to be a bit too melodramatic for most people's tastes. Em'ly is still the innocent young girl who can muster only a frail defense when Miss Dartle shames her. Em'ly pleads for forgiveness and explains how much she has suffered because of her passion for Steerforth.

CHAPTERS 51-52

Summary

The next morning, Mr. Peggotty tells David and his aunt about Em'ly's escape from Littimer. Em'ly had run along the beach until she fell down with exhaustion, and when she awoke, there was a woman leaning over her. The woman recognized Em'ly and took her home, where she cared for her and arranged for Em'ly to sail to France.

In France, Em'ly "took service to wait on travelling ladies at an inn," but one day she saw "that snake" (either Steerforth or Littimer), and she immediately left for England. She had wanted to go directly to Yarmouth, but she was afraid that Mr. Peggotty had not forgiven her, so she went to London. Here she met a woman whom she thought was a friend but who was really about to lead Em'ly into a life of prostitution. Before Em'ly could be harmed, Martha found her and "brought her safe out."

Mr. Peggotty makes plans to go to Australia with Em'ly to begin a new life. The next morning, Mr. Peggotty and David go to Yarmouth to prepare for the departure, and David visits Mr. Omer at his shop. The old tailor is paralyzed and is in a wheelchair, but is in the best of spirits. He says that he has read David's book and tells him how proud he is to have known him and his family.

David continues on to the Peggotty house where Mr. Peggotty is packing for the voyage. Ham asks David to write to Em'ly for him and to tell her to forgive him for pressing his affections upon her. Ham feels that, if he had not had her promise to marry him, she might have confided her troubles to him and that then he could have saved her.

Before Mr. Peggotty locks the door on the old boat for the last time, Mrs. Gummidge begs him to let her go with him and Em'ly on their trip. Mr. Peggotty gives in to her request, and the next morning, they leave for London to begin the long journey to Australia.

David and Mr. Dick prepare to leave for Canterbury for the mysterious meeting arranged by Mr. Micawber. Dora insists that she can manage quite well until their return and that Miss Betsey should go with them. Tommy Traddles also accompanies them on the trip. Micawber tells them to call at the office of Wickfield and Heep and ask for Miss Wickfield.

The somewhat confused group proceeds to the office as directed and asks to see Agnes Wickfield. Mr. Micawber leads them into Mr. Wickfield's former office and they meet Mr. Heep, who is surprised at their presence. Despite his usual nervous, slimy manner, Uriah attempts to play the "gracious" host; however, when Agnes joins them, Mr. Micawber begins to berate the clerk for his trickery. Micawber, in a grandiose manner, proceeds to expose Uriah Heep by reading a detailed account of his crimes against the firm, Mr. Wickfield, and Micawber himself. The proof is quite substantial (a notebook that Uriah thought he had destroyed), yet the cowardly villain admits nothing and merely utters counterthreats hoping to deter the proceedings. Mrs. Heep keeps telling her son to be "umble," but Uriah realizes that this will no longer work. In fact, Uriah is quite beside himself when his mother, quite unwittingly, substantiates several of the charges.

When all the facts are made known, Miss Trotwood joins the attack. She seizes Heep by the collar and demands that money which she invested be returned to her (she had previously blamed herself for the loss because she didn't want to hurt Mr. Wickfield's feelings, but now she realizes Uriah was "the consummate villain"). Once David succeeds in calming his aunt, Traddles takes over the matter and tells Uriah that he must make reparations for all his dishonest dealings or be sent to prison.

Quite satisfied with his brilliant performance, Micawber is even further delighted to be reunited with his family. Again he is hopeful that "something will turn up" and he is thrilled when Miss Trotwood suggests that she can "loan" him the funds necessary for him and his family to accompany Mr. Peggotty to Australia. Micawber is certain that it will be just the thing and that "something of an extraordinary nature will turn up on that shore."

Commentary

In Chapter 50, Dickens turns to Em'ly's redemption; this can only be realized when she rejects the last symbol of sophistication—that is, her knowledge of foreign languages. Littimer told David that Em'ly picked up the language quite well and had become, to all appearances, a "lady." But now Mr. Peggotty says that "the language of that country was quite gone from her." He says that finally the child of the woman with whom she was staying called her a "fisherman's daughter," and that Em'ly understood and began to cry. Only then was Em'ly able to begin her journey back home—cured of her "illness."

Dora's illness in Chapter 42, in contrast, is treated lightly, although it is obvious that David is deeply troubled about it.

In contrast to the collapse of Uriah Heep, two other characters reach their peak. Mr. Micawber reveals a serious side by his efforts to collect evidence, and a nobleness of character by his willingness to accept poverty rather than continue to live in the deceitful web spun by Uriah Heep. He even succeeds in putting his flowery eloquence to good use in the composition and the delivery of his letter. Traddles is also outstanding in the affair. David is sorry that he didn't recognize his former classmate's true character and capabilities before this.

CHAPTERS 53-54

Summary

David remembers back to the time of his wife's death after Dora had been ill for some time. In fact, David cannot remember when she was *not* sick. David noticed that Jip, Dora's dog, had become quite old and pathetically feeble, just like his mistress. Dora tells David to write a letter to Agnes asking her to come, and David does so. One night shortly after Agnes' arrival, Dora tells David that she was too young to marry and that perhaps it might have been better if she and David had "loved each other as a boy and girl, and forgotten it." She sends David downstairs and bids farewell by saying, "It is much better as it is."

David sits in his chair beside the fireplace while Jip lies on the floor beside him. David's thoughts wander to what Dora has said, and he cannot help thinking that perhaps Dora was correct in her remark. At that moment, Jip comes to him and whines to go upstairs. David tells the dog: "Not to-night, Jip . . . it may be never again." Thereupon, Jip lies down and "with a plaintive cry is dead." At this exact moment, Agnes comes downstairs, "full of pity and . . . grief." David knows that Dora, too, is dead.

David is very distressed over Dora's death, and Agnes suggests that he go abroad in order to forget his unhappiness. She makes all the arrangements, but David must wait until after "the final pulverization of Heep" and until the emigrants leave.

The emigration of the Micawber family is to be financed by Miss Trotwood, who has regained her money. Traddles explains that he went over the Wickfield accounts and found that the business was not short of funds and that Miss Betsey's money would be returned, except for two thousand pounds that she had withdrawn some years before. Miss Betsey informs David that she didn't tell him about this nest egg because she wanted to see if he could get along without her financial help. Miss Betsey also agrees to pay Mr. Micawber's IOU's as they are now due, and Mr. Micawber can repay her after he makes good in Australia. Agnes decides to open a school so she can take care of her father now that his business has been liquidated. Traddles reports that Uriah embezzled the money because of his hatred for David, and that now Heep and his mother have gone to London, but that "if he could do us, or any of us, any injury or annoyance, no doubt he would."

Miss Trotwood is distressed by something all this time, but David doesn't know what it is. Finally, his aunt asks him to go for a ride in the morning, and she will tell him the reason. They drive to a London hospital where a hearse is waiting with the body of her missing husband. He died a few days before, and Miss Betsey notes that "Six-and-thirty years ago, this day, my dear . . . I was married. God forgive us all."

Commentary

Dickens has often been taken to task by the critics for the very overdone scene which is the key focus of Chapter 53; neither the death of David's mother nor that of Barkis contains as much pathos, but it must be said in Dickens' defense that Dora shows more maturity and practicality than she has ever shown before. Her analysis of their inept marriage is accurate, and she exhibits a deep understanding of David's inclinations by inviting Agnes to be with her at the end.

In Chapter 54, Dickens begins to tie up the threads of his far-flung plots. Heep is disgraced and removed to London; the Micawbers and Mr. Peggotty are removed even further, to Australia; and Miss Betsey's fortune is saved and her husband buried. The minor characters are being dispensed with so that David's life will again become the focus of the reader's attention.

68

CHAPTERS 55-56

Summary

David has written to Em'ly at Ham's request and in the return letter, she asks him to thank Ham for his kindness and bid him farewell. David decides that since he has a few days before the emigrants' ship leaves, he will go to Yarmouth and deliver the note to Ham personally. On the way to Yarmouth a great storm begins to break. He spends the night at the old inn in Yarmouth and during the night the rain and wind grow stronger. David joins the townspeople as they watch the raging sea and then he goes to find Ham, but discovers that Ham is out repairing someone's ship. David returns to the inn and after a fitful night he is awakened by shouts from someone outside his door that a ship is wrecked down on the beach. He rushes to the scene and sees the schooner being battered to destruction by the wind and waves. One mast is broken off and the sailors onboard are trying to cut that part away. Several of the seamen are washed overboard to their death and only a single, curly-haired man remains alive on the foundering vessel. David then sees Ham running through the crowd on shore and knows that he is going to try to reach the ship. David attempts to restrain him, but Ham has some men tie rope around him and he swims out to the wreck. Ham never makes it aboard, however, for a huge wave breaks up the ship. When they draw in the rope, Ham is dead. Ham's body is carried to a nearby house, and David stays there until a fisherman comes and tells him to look at the other body that has washed ashore. It is that of Steerforth. "I saw him lying with his head upon his arm, as I had often seen him lie at school."

David realizes that his feelings for his friend have never really changed; he has always loved and admired Steerforth no matter what he has done. David knows that it is his responsibility to tell Mrs. Steerforth of her son's death and to return the body for burial. It is some time before Mrs. Steerforth realizes that David is reporting her son's death. Rosa Dartle then launches a vehement attack on Mrs. Steerforth, blaming her for the misfortune, and proclaiming her own love for Steerforth. Mrs. Steerforth goes into a state of shock, and Miss Dartle begins to cry and tenderly tries to comfort her.

Commentary

The most outlandish coincidence of all occurs in this chapter, but the description of the storm overshadows everything else, and one almost forgets the improbability of Steerforth's appearance because the climax is so startling. In Chapter 56, Dickens resolves the entire Steerforth story—Steerforth is dead, not as a direct result of his dissolute habits, but as if Nature had taken a hand in exacting payment for the harm he has done; Rosa Dartle is revealed as an embittered, rejected worshipper of Steerforth, whom she had continued to love unrecognized and unrequited ever since their childhood; Mrs. Steerforth, already an invalid, is reduced to shock by the news of her son's death—another instance of Dickens' penchant for visiting poetic justice on undeserving characters.

CHAPTERS 57-58

Summary

David decides to keep the news of Steerforth's tragic death from Mr. Peggotty and Em'ly. He enlists the aid of Mr. Micawber, who agrees (with characteristic flourish and oratory) to keep newspaper reports from reaching the group before they sail. David wants Mr. Peggotty and Em'ly to depart "in happy ignorance" for their new life in Australia.

David, his aunt, Agnes, and Clara Peggotty see them off, and David joyfully discovers that Martha Endell will accompany the group to Australia. Mrs. Micawber rounds up her children and recites her promise never to desert her husband. The ship begins to move and David waves goodbye to Em'ly and Mr. Peggotty standing arm-in-arm as the ship pulls away.

David then leaves England and spends three years traveling around the world. His sorrow over the loss of his wife increases daily, unrelieved by his journeys to different countries.

David receives a packet of letters from Agnes while he is in Switzerland in which she tells David that his sorrow must be his strength so that he can turn "affliction to good." David intensely returns to his writing and sends a story to Traddles, who acts as an agent for David. David's fame continues to grow, and he finally

70

begins his third work of fiction. His mind begins to clear and his health improves. He decides to return to England.

Commentary

Chapter 57 provides a welcome relief from the sadness and the pathos of the preceding sections. Dickens provides the reader with emotional variety and also shows that life goes on in the face of tragedy.

The shipboard scene is very effective. The ship's passengers, like the Micawbers and the Peggottys, are all seeking a new start. This optimism on the part of downtrodden, weary, and dispossessed people helps end the chapter on a happy note and conveys Dickens' firm belief in the inevitable triumph of good.

In Chapter 58, we see that David's special thoughts are still about Agnes. He realizes that he loves her, but he thinks that they will never be able to marry because of the brother-sister relationship that exists between them. These thoughts plague David's mind as he prepares to return home.

CHAPTERS 59-60

Summary

David returns to London on a wintry autumn evening and he plans to surprise his friends, who do not expect him until Christmas. At Gray's Inn Coffee-house, David asks a waiter about "Mr. Traddles' . . . reputation among the lawyers," but the waiter doesn't seem to know Tommy's name, and David begins to worry about his friend's position.

Eventually, David finds Traddles' apartment and discovers that he is now married to Sophy, whom he courted for so long. Sophy's five sisters are living with them, but the family seems happy, and David is convinced that Traddles will succeed in his law practice.

David returns to the coffee house and notices Mr. Chillip, the old family doctor, seated in a corner. Mr. Chillip doesn't recognize him at first, but after David reintroduces himself they talk about Mr. Murdstone (now Mr. Chillip's neighbor) and how he has driven his second wife "all but melancholy mad." When David talks about Miss Betsey Trotwood, the doctor hurries off to bed "as if he were not quite safe anywhere else." (Clearly, he remembers, in David's words, the "Dragon.")

When David arrives at Miss Trotwood's cottage, he is "received with open arms" by his aunt, Mr. Dick, and their new housekeeper—Peggotty. The happy group is together once more.

David and his aunt stay up very late and talk, primarily about Agnes. David asks if she has acquired any suitors, and Miss Betsey replies that she could have married twenty times but she seems to have a special "attachment." His aunt will tell him no more because it is only a suspicion on her part.

In the morning, David travels by horseback to Canterbury to see Agnes. At the house, David and Agnes are joyfully reunited. David finds that he cannot tell Agnes of his great love for her, and she proceeds to talk about her school and her quiet life with her father. When David asks about her "attachment," she becomes evasive, and David lets the topic drop. Mr. Wickfield relates the story of his marriage and the mistakes he has made in his past; however, he praises Agnes and compares her affectionate and gentle heart to her mother's broken one. Later, David is able to tell Agnes of his gratefulness to her for all her help.

When David rides back at night, all his memories go with him. He fears that Agnes is unhappy . . . and he knows in his heart that he is too.

Commentary

Very little happens to David in Chapter 59. Dickens uses the device of having David be told about the happenings of various characters. Very quickly the various loose ends of the story are being picked up and tucked away in these last few chapters. Agnes, perhaps, is the only person who has remained unchanged throughout the course of the novel. Her blend of sense, sympathy, and motherly affection are enduring qualities that transcend the physical existence of things.

CHAPTERS 61-62

Summary

David receives such a large volume of mail because of his writing that he decides to have Traddles manage his correspondence from London. In particular, David and Traddles discuss a letter that has arrived from Mr. Creakle, the former Salem House proprietor. He is now a magistrate who runs a model prison and the two young men decide to visit him. As Traddles and David are escorted through the building, Mr. Creakle explains that each prisoner is isolated so that they may all be restored to a "wholesome state of mind, leading to sincere contrition and repentance." Mr. Creakle is very proud of two of his model prisoners, Numbers Twenty-Seven and Twenty-eight. David is amazed to find that they are *Uriah Heep* and *Littimer*! Uriah is in jail for fraud, forgery, and conspiracy, and when he sees David he sanctimoniously "forgives" David for being "violent" to him and warns him to mend his ways. Littimer was imprisoned for robbing his master, and David learns that he would have escaped had it not been for Miss Mowcher, the dwarf hairdresser.

David frequently visits Agnes to read her parts of his novel-in-progress. All the time he is with Agnes, he thinks of how much he loves her and what a perfect wife she would be.

Shortly after Christmas, Aunt Betsey tells David that Agnes is about to be married. This rouses David to action, and he rides out to see Agnes to break down the barrier "with a determined hand." Agnes is very reluctant to talk about her "attachment" and she begins to cry. David hesitantly professes his intentions and Agnes tells him that he is the only person she has ever loved. Two weeks later they are married.

The wedding is a very simple affair and the only guests are Traddles, Sophy, and Dr. Strong and his wife. After the ceremony, Agnes tells David that the night Dora died, she told Agnes that only she should "occupy this vacant place."

Commentary

Chapter 61 offers a brief interlude from David's romantic problems, and it gives Dickens a chance to comment on prison reform. Although Dickens did not believe in excessive brutality, neither did he condone "soft" treatment for inmates. David, you should note, is *very* cynical about the "model" prison.

At long last, the long "blind-man's-bluff" romance between Agnes and David is finally resolved in Chapter 62. David finally realizes who it is that he *really* loves; this is a coup for Dickens; his main character realizes what the reader has hoped for all along.

CHAPTERS 63-64

Summary

David and Agnes have been married for ten years when one night an old man calls on them. It is Mr. Peggotty, who has now returned to England for a brief visit. He tells David how his little band of emigrants have prospered in Australia by raising livestock. Em'ly has had many chances to marry but she has refused them all and is content to stay with her uncle. Martha Endell is married, and even Mrs. Gummidge could have married, but she rejected her suitor rather firmly by hitting him with a bucket. Mr. Micawber has become a noted District Magistrate, and David reads a news account of a dinner in his honor in which the toastmaster was none other than Doctor Mell, David's former teacher.

Mr. Peggotty stays with David for nearly a month and before he leaves he visits Ham's grave. He asks David to copy the plain inscription on the tablet and then he gathers up a tuft of grass from the grave, and a little earth, "for Em'ly."

David looks back on his life and tells the reader about his old friends—almost like a theater curtain call. Aunt Betsey is older, but unchanged, and is cared for by Peggotty. Mr. Dick continues to work on his writing and to fly his kites. Mrs. Steerforth and Rosa Dartle still live together and grieve over their loss. Julia Mills, Dora's old friend, is married to a wealthy Scot and is unhappy. Traddles is a Magistrate and he and Sophy have two boys who are being educated at the best schools and are distinguishing themselves as scholars. Dr. Strong labors on his Dictionary (somewhere around the letter "D"), and Jack Maldon sneers at the world and thinks Doctor Strong "charmingly antique." Justice has won out.

The happiest of all is David. His love for Agnes is complete. "The dear presence, without which I were nothing, bears me company." His only wish is that she will continue to live with him and that when he dies, she will be near him, "pointing upward."

Commentary

These final two chapters are often called in today's vernacular, the author's anticlimactic "mopping-up" operation. Dickens disposes of all the remaining characters, and we see that his faith remains in the superiority of good and its eventual triumph over evil. This was a dictum that Dickens inserted into every one of his novels.

SELECTED BIBLIOGRAPHY

CHESTERTON, GILBERT KEITH. *Charles Dickens.* New York: Schocken Books, 1965.

FIELDING, K. J. *Charles Dickens: A Critical Introduction.* New York: David McKay Co., 1958.

FORSTER, JOHN. *The Life of Charles Dickens*, 2 vols. New York: E. P. Dutton, 1928.

HOUSE, HUMPHRY. *The Dickens World*, 2nd ed. New York: Oxford University Press, 1960.

JOHNSON, EDGAR. *Charles Dickens: His Tragedy and Triumph.* New York: Simon and Schuster, 1953.

LEY, J. W. T. *The Dickens Circle.* London: Chapman and Hall, 1919.

MILLER, J. HILLIS. *Charles Dickens: The World of His Novels.* Cambridge, Massachusetts: Harvard University Press, 1959.

NISBET, ADA. *Dickens and Ellen Ternan.* Berkeley: University of California Press, 1952.

ORWELL, GEORGE. *Dickens, Dali, and Others.* New York: Harcourt, Brace, 1946.

PEARSON, HESKETH. *Dickens: His Character, Comedy, and Career.* New York: Harper and Brothers, 1949.

VAN GHENT, DOROTHY. *The English Novel: Form and Function.* New York: Holt, Rinehart and Winston, 1953.

NOTES

NOTES

NOTES

NOTES

NOTES

NOTES